Bells of Freedom

when agony finds its words......

DEBABRATA MAULIK

First Published in January 2019

ISBN: 978-93-5347-102-6

BLUE ROSE PUBLISHERS
www.bluerosepublishers.com
info@bluerosepublishers.com
+91 8882 898 898

Cover Design:
Mohit Joshi

Typographic Design:
Teena Maurya

Distributed by: Blue Rose, Amazon, Flipkart, Shopclues

This book, a Commentary on Humanity & Emotion, Society & Environment and an Anthology of Social pain and agony is dedicated to my beloved fellow citizen

Prelude

Twenty first century India has been undergoing turmoil and detestation. Civilised human being is finding difficulties in pursuing civility. A huge wall made of hate, hunger, malnutrition and deprivation is standing before them. To these are added man-made atrocities. Common people are finding it to be an uphill task to cross over the wall. Like Jalianwala there are guns and mortars of freak and untruth salvo being fired in every direction. In the midst of these manmade chaos people are still surviving. I salute our people for observing patience in spite of many pain and agony that have been caused to them. It has been easy for me to understand their feeling because I am one of them. These poetries have been a spontaneous outcome of my mind as and whenever I have thought of my fellow citizen, their life and happiness, emotion and the enormous impending damages in the environment and ecology.

These untold misery and agony of hundreds thousands of human being have been given expression in this book in the form of poetries. They have become the backbone of a commentary on Humanity, Emotion, Society and Environment. This compilation of poetries is being handed over to you under the book titled ***"Bells of Freedom"***. I would be honoured if it influence your mind even for a fraction of a second and make you think of the ambient we are living today. Have we ever thought of this mother land for which martyrs laid down their lives so that we live in an independent country and common people withstood irreplaceable losses? Is this the state of affairs we dreamt of when we were in our dream hood? Obviously it is not. My book of poetry should for a while bring in fresh air into our mind and thoughts enabling us thinking on our own for a new Dawn. Let your wishes find the road to a *New Dawn*.

Index

Environment

Our Past

There are kingdoms, no king rules
There are palaces, no human lives
Empty palaces thence gave cover
Are now falling to human desire

There are rivers, no water flow
Lands dried up water table low
Farmers thence reap green harvest
Now give in to modern city thirst

There are hills, no tree stands there
Hill tops wide open no ice to cover
Folks thence played with glacier water
Now playing with guns and mortar

There are forests, no one rests there
Scant trees look no longer greener
Animals thence hide in sun shadows
Now left for neighbourhood gallows

There are lush lands but lying barren
Ripe crops often hit by natural siren
Poor remuneration crippled farmers
Now left to end life in debt-trap disaster

Morning wakes me up bring no peace
Prepare me for another hectic cease
Time pass glimpse in past recollection
Now fill my soul with exasperation

My Disappearance

You may call me a messenger
I deliver messages to a stranger
Once I was known as Runner
Time altered my name to courier

Vast network of offices exist there
Connect people of the state entire
Every single house used to wait
Eagerly for his visit once at least

His visit is always sought after
Arriving letter cheer up the receiver
Today a few expect him to arrive
Delivering message for a surprise

Postal set-up struggle to survive
It will not be late when it goes quiet
Toll rising rapidly by cell phone entry
Postman stop visit by the century

A colossal loss it would bring
Such a set-up seeing grounding
One day the messenger will vanish
This age serve costly courier dish

How to be a Human Being

Northern breeze cools my body
My head springs up unsteady
I give my cloth to a roadside poor
Try to be a human being for sure

People would elect me as a leader
I would carry out people welfare
Country would start believing
Wish to see in me a human being

Irrational beast kills for living
Rational men kill for score settling
Being similar both put life at stake
Human wisdom refuses me to take

Hate untruth wins the occasion
Conspiracy shrewdness holds on
Human life turns a shattered sting
Prevent me to be a human being

Poor unable in meeting both ends
Lack of compassion hurts
People suffer owing indifference
Scold me I do not suit human race

It is difficult to be a human being
In spite of probing logical reasoning
Right in the midst of mankind
I cannot chase unconcern bind

In search of Sunshine

Where do I find sunshine tell me Lord
I crave for it in my urban board
High scrapper blocks the Sun
Tall trees shadow it on my plan

Warped escalation of low hutments
Grown as bye product of progress
Poisonous air deflect my mind
All needed sunshine I never find

Twisted natives stench my ambient
People never withstand foul scent
Finding hard to come out open
I may not ever find my sunshine

I fly to mountain I fly to sea shore
In search of my sunshine I adore
I visit village I ride my boat
Foul River spoils my moment

In today's world we remain busy
We do not find time to be picky
Seriousness kills the daily rhythm
Away from sunshine we mime

I love sunshine looking for it
Upper floor provides enough of it
Country chasing sunshine hymn
There is none to provide paradigm

Call it History

A chronology of events of the past
Some are good some are worst
Today becomes past on tomorrow
It adds to the power of sorrow
History create itself men propagate
You win or lose times take a note

Kings and emperors pursue citizens
Some ruled kingdom as servants
A few being slayer, a few nurturer
Time happily record both deed their
Ruled not aiming to create own tale
Intellectuals stored it for foretell

Some Kings has no place in record
None remembers them to be graced
Modern time created a privileged few
These destroy more than they grew
Believes in being served than serving
For securing claps from ignored being

Neither in our hand nor we write future
People do remember events for sure
Events as has crushed them or butchered
Time record perceive them much angered
Such actions become part of history
Time passed by ensued age read the story

Blood carrying river changed his heart
Turning warrior Ashok becoming a saint
People remember this in ancient diary
As it affected the mankind in entirety
Killing innocent men women in anger
Affected society record it for the future

Cleansing

Wind has presented autumn in the air
I was passing by the lane slower
A tree spreading smell of autumn flower
The fragrance soaked me all over
Ahead was lying the main cross road
At the very point I soon reached
The corner waste bin emitting foul smell
So bad it wiped off my aroma all
Frequent stenches remind every second
Country is failed to be cleaned
A spotless state comes with clean soul
Dry jingle do not clean the bowel
Autumns will continue to come and go
But bad odour would flow too
Promises fail with no execution bin
My soul search fresh air clean

Misplaced Expedition

All washed away in the flood water
Not even leave out my small hut
I can't build my dream play house
On the ingest shore of my pain

Colossal deforestation weaken hold
Big mountain split on the road
I can't build my dream play house
On the devastated path of my pain

Greatly demoralised social culture
Left mothers and wives weeping
I can't build my dream play house
On the broken soul of my pain

Sullied thoughts widely preached
Left young minds despoiled
I can't build my dream play house
On the uncertain future of my pain

Heartless attitude to food producers
Calamity wrath annihilate them
I can't build my dream play house
On the remorse of my pain

The Earthquake

This day years ago there was an earthquake
Human moral present and future did shake
People were served a swine's paradigm
Fate took them to a sudden social mayhem
Queues of heads stood with begging bowl
Awaiting their turn to regain broken soul
That was earthquake of despair and anxiety
Making people unable to stand for unity
Loss of wealth put many in disadvantage
Social crooks made fortune of coinage
That was a severe blow on the sovereignty
Unscrupulous make merry of people's pity
Earthquake comes never in isolation
Put the society in to a trail of devastation
It will take long time to replenish the loss
God thrust earthquake as new social fuss
Huge misery percolates in the society
Twisted mind succeeds in their tricks dirty

Life
&
Truth

Our Life

Calm evening sitting by the side of the sea
Incessant waves break on the shrine steps
Hears the holy sound of the temple bell
She puts her lamp on the sea tail
Pushing away waves she keeps lamp afloat
Consecutive waves however return it
Like life wishing each day to be rewarding
Destiny provide way to be disappointing

Cool morning put us on the wing
Racing wind under blue sky puffing
Winter break brings cheer in sight
In open air young boy flying his kite
Managing wind he tries its even sway
Unfriendly wind however takes it other way
Like life setting up its future for creation
Fate provide the way of distraction

Chasing autumn

As I enter platform train was rolling away
Stuck and stranded my plan falling array
Job letter in one hand luggage in the other
A strong urge pushed me to run after
Finally threw myself in to the last coach
I boarded the train and began my chase

Moving from old place to a new one
Pursued ride from old job to fresh one
One summer after another gone by
My chase continued as time flew by
Sometime money sometime fame
Provoked me to run after my fate

Not knowing where it would take me
One summer continued to chase another
Settling my life becomes a distant reign
Dream strikes often as if chasing my train
One day an autumn would find my destiny
That would stop my chasing mutiny

Dilemma of a Father

Child walks by holding father's finger
Enjoys riding a horse played by his father
It is the bond that weaves the connection
This pious bond enjoys eternal affiliation

It is the finest moment in the life of a father
To be a horse to his little kid's pleasure
Man not being a father misses this sensation
Would wonder about a father's emotion

A farmer wishes his son to be a farmer
Feel grown up son will assist in future
Son grows confused in the earthy ambient
Father's dilemma search for right sentiment

Long wait for his return from work
Keep awake the father along the dark
Daunting worries put the father in quandary
Who is not a father overlooks this misery

Many agonies happiness and ecstasy
Are wonderful moments of a father's fancy
Who is not a father is deprived of the experience
Feeling of compassion can never be his essence

Human being when robbed of emotion
Misplaces his heart with suspicion
What is left in him is jealousy and commotion
He finds devils hand in all his action

Drums of autumn

In the clear blue sky white clouds floating
Like cotton clusters whitened by ginning
A few grey clouds presents black patch
Autumn declare arrival in cool catch

First beat of drum make me nostalgic
I indulge in the noise of autumn chaotic
Warmth of puja festivities fills happiness
Drums of autumn calm in togetherness

Autumn drums make me home bound
It is also time mind wish to go around
Mountains and sea seek our company
Historical sites also dance in symphony

In the tune of drums my mind dance
Make me move one to next trance
Creating many great moments of life
Nostalgic autumn drum play to recite

Warmest Place

In the midst of tall mountains around
We stood on a small green top ground
Blowing cold air diminish in the valley
Making it the right place for assembly
Team put up our camp for the night
Sitting in a ring we soak in bonfire light
Warmth of the fire came as God's grace
To all of us it was the warmest place
Thousand miles away from our home
All we made our new cozy warm abode
Night passed by the early morning ray
We spent a memorable night far away
It was the warmest place in my heart
Bright as Sunlight warms my guts

Flowers

You seat on the dear one's tomb
Someone had watered you long
Sharing you with one's love
You feel privileged here

You seat on the God's feet here
Pilgrim has placed you there
Putting faith in God through you
You bridge the sacred vow

You lie soaked in the water tank
Perfumer has brought you there
Waiting to create aroma to share
You spread fragrance and care

You glow up from the branch tier
Best place nature sent you there
Whispering in the air to pollinate
You make possible new life create

You are not the God

You are everywhere people say
I travel places to see you as I may
Find your insensitive act but not you
Among them waiting in long queue

The sage engages in tireless preaching
For keeping rational thirst soothing
Not making any difference in reality
Life continues with obscurity

My God never lies that I believe
I have faith that he would not deceive
Deprived getting poorer the rich richer
That you are not God make me wonder

God cannot be heartless ruthless
No longer tolerate penance of penniless
He appears rescuing downtrodden
Strike me your absence amongst broken

Helping fellow people earns devotion
Using them pushes to rejection
Foreseeing common happiness in them
Let us be Human first to avoid shame

Teacher is the God to the student
Children find the God in their Parent
Citizens find the rescuer in the Leader
Mankind sees peace in the Conciliator

Forgotten Village

Forgotten when I visited a village last
May be then I was a boy or an infant
Mother took me to the village school
Crossing the muddy road and pool
Young eyes were grasping with wonder
How different those world were
Trying to free from mother's clutch
Grip gets tighter as school approach

Recall green landscape filled with sapling,
Swinging in step with wind as if nodding
Sprint under blue sky along the alley in field
I breathe the fragrance of the mystic mud
An unknown aroma dragged me there
Villager making molasses from cane sugar
These were not there in my town
Where I was born and grown

My autumn now long for visiting a village
Making me scared as I became a town age
I may not find a village as I remember
Discontent would have pained me sharper
Muddy roads have given way to concrete
Weak bamboo huts to brick abode
Farmer's green field given way to factory
Buying food from the Malls is modern story

This was not what I wished for once
Before I made my learning parlance
My village would have its independent life
In line with what we have here our city life
This progress men did not wished early
Thy name development came harshly
Vital produce once grown in our village
Are now replaced by foreign grain age

Person never change

Mountain looks up river flows downhill
Cloud floats on shower pour still
Sprout springs up piercing root down soil
Dwelling stand up water stored in well
Natural phenomena they are all
They all change that is truth eternal

Human being takes birth grow forth
Looks up the sky standing on base firth
A childhood blossom into youth
Ideal heroism convictions find its path
Blooming a mind that never reciprocate
It all open out as life renovate

Person accustom with life to suffer
Fitting self to suit varied state of affair
Friendship fights with camaraderie
Brotherhoods do not give in chivalry
Mind gives up before ego making resolute
Person never change remain definite

Situation force actor to change manner
But actor carry on acting that not alter
Greed force cheater amend cheating skill
But cheater persist cheating not to spill
Lucidity force leader mend his shady practice
But leader keep on sham that not to cease

Mother's Grief

She was still sitting, staring at her door
Her little boy is to return home from far
For his footstep she tunes her keen ears
Such long delay never happened earlier

The morning was cool and shining
Boy went to school with eyes all beaming
School sits without a Morning Prayer
To our children this may not matter

Came noon bringing a gang of unruly
Along came violence making life disorderly
Disruption invited uncalled firing
Hitting a child cutting short his gleaming

Mother waits for her son's return home
But God has altered plan for some
That a lamp has burnt out so early
One would know Mother's grief surely

Soldier

A soldier is born within first
It is born out of the inner call of self trust
A mind flourishes love for motherland
Nothing so pure than native land
Slowly turning inner urge into craving
Protect the motherland by self-sacrificing

Mind nurtured in the midst of honesty
Bringing home embellishments with purity
Patriotic mind lives among soldiers
As if it has fastened orange covers
Family disseminate commitment and trust
Soldiers with blue colour emerge fast

Let them live in their whims for sacrifice
We not impede in their passion suffice
Their obedient world is pious and great
Promoted by honest calls of their heart
They are scared of leaders' provocation
It is beyond their disciplined perception

True soldier begins their homework early
Get rid of communality hatred equally
Temple, Mosques, Churches spread fragrance
Reap in mind the essence of semblance
Creating trustful spiritual united ambiance
Soldiers of all faith readies for sacrifice

Barbed Wire

Surrounded by cliffs on mountain ridge
Below a great valley that is in siege
Flowing river one side, a fence on the other
The village is bounded by barbed wire
It is my village my sweet home lies there
I grew up there spending many years

Come full moon night heard animals howl
Mother used to narrate stories I recall
Soon I hear the young mother sheep's cry
Watchful shepherd dog befall wolf's try
None can come as there is barbed wire
Secured I fall sleep on the lap of mother

Far from my village here I was sitting
Midnight I hear chasing crowd shouting
They are perhaps running after an offender
A class created out of the deprived sufferer
Society remain apathetic to human need
There is no barbed wire to get them shield

Killers of human being roaming freely
State looks the other way shamelessly
Innocent commoners moving with fear
Threatened by suspicion and terror
Wonder in the middle what stored ahead
There is no barbed wire to get them shield

Lord! What are you made of?

Oh Lord! Wondering your presence unseen
Seeing weak toddler mother weeps within
Chronic malnutrition taking its toll
I do not find you there to console

Sign of worries seen on mother's face
Waiting long for return of her girl safe
Anti-socials becoming desperate each day
I do not find you there with mother to pray

Soldiers' parents losing heart every day
Our border killing increases day by day
Warmonger mindset is taking its toll each day
I do not find you there with parents to pray

Mourning farmers besieged with fears
Storm rain has spoiled their standing crops
Inability of repaying loans cast on shadow
I do not find you there amidst farmer's sorrow

Oh Lord! I wonder where forth you stride
Wherever you are be honest in drive
Feel sympathetic with human difficulties
I do not find you exist among the worries

My happy times

Rain has stopped given way to blue sky
Floating white clouds as if they fly
Grass flowers waving high by the river slate
Boatman sings autumn standing on the gate
Sometime ago flood devastated them
It could not snatch their smile and fame
It is time for Puja celebration
For which we plan with exhilaration

This is our happy time we remember
Rickshaw tour flashing childhood reminder
Visiting Pandals and relatives customary
Evenings spent in adventure armory
Lights glamour affected adolescent mind
Seeing known face in new dress did bind
Unlucky few were away from the taste of joy
That were the happy times we did enjoy

Mourning time

When dear one die of deceases
It is mourning time for relatives
When passerby die on the road
No tears forth come there to shed
When thousands die of a riot
Monarchy feels shy of respite
Appear battle of hatred has won
At the cost of a divided nation

The time of mourning of unlucky
The perpetuators engage in gaiety
Society looks up to find motive
Lacks courage to force a plebiscite
Life continues with scars in heart
Human memory does live short
Society waits for future anarchism
In search of a fresh mourning time

Hope

To hope is nature we all wish
Cries of baby hoping to draw our notice
Dog bark hoping to get his feed
Hoping for customer shopkeepers heed

To hope is nature we all do
Every moment pass with a wish or two
Hoping to see light at the end of the tunnel
Most hopes see through the channel

To hope is nature we all see
Anticipation drives human sea
All wish to succeed student or stars
Leaders as well the social reformers

To hope is nature we all react
Hopes guided by greed fall flat
Arrogance make hope sounds empty
Boastful hope allows falling pity

Hope falls flat on cowards
It carries remorse to hundreds
Virtuous hope always finds success
Society imbibe to honesty access

Let us hope the Sun would shine
We renew our hope to be benign
Treat fellow men with dignity
Sure we would achieve sovereignty

Truth
&
Conflict

Hatred

Enduring distress created me in solitude
You inherited me in warm fortitude
Pessimistic surrounding brings me up
Contagiously I spread my wings sharp

Clairvoyant loved me hand folded
Kept me mounting inside stretched
Enabling me surfacing on a later day
At whims and whisper of fired hay

Provoking people to be prejudiced
Ugliness travel faster raising its head
Blood spill there downing lives
I win reaching the helm of minds

People reward my perpetuator
I come back at every need there
Happily embracing double speaking
Disguised I keep floating my wing

Arrogance

I live on pride and intolerance
Aligning my thoughts in parlance
Jealousy is my companion
Only to bias mind orientation

I grow on human psycho fancy
Following the art of bigotry
Sycophant is my friend
It is my alleyway I defend

I spread my wings of abhorrence
Justifying there my presence
As ambience gets thorny and pert
I switch to preaching moral cart

Confronting minds feel scary
Justifying the act of disorderly
Intolerance surface in violation
I compromise ethics and speculation

Aimless evolution cause wound
But I remain supercilious hound
New slogan do not change the story
Budding people lead by old trajectory

Hesitation

A state of mind I visit you often
Stop your thought in action domain
All in a while unmindfully
Shifting from one to other quickly

I may harm more than helping
May form a habit if allowed growing
Oh dear then follow your guts
You get rid of me before it hurts

Due to me Generals lost many wars
Dubious kings their kingdoms
Travelers have lost their direction
And many nations their progression

Gracefully spoken lies succeed often
Dithering truths fail time and again
Civility loses its true relevance
In the current humanity of ignorance

Great indecision leads delayed feat
Conscious wavering creates defeat
Failing to provide stable guarantee
Perplexed nation submit to incredulity

Ignorance

I am bliss for illiterate ones
Work hand in hand with arrogance
Some pretention outdo my presence
Hurts belief making low my confidence
Leading to defiance again and again
Secure clapping for personal gain
Unknowingly bent upon to astray
Great civilisation stands to disarray

Because of my presence in countless
Unscrupulous do wrong in all easiness
Thrusting its mischievous thoughts
Ignite passion leading to immoral roads
Natural ways of coming out of ignorance
Gets sealed inside the human essence
Ignorance prosper on the country's soil
Deceivers survive protecting their trail

Ignorant unknown about wrong doing
Hardships put bleeding hearts to crying
Arrogance superseding the common sense
Not knowing basic welfare of citizens
Deceived people sacrifice beautiful today
For the misery of unknown future day
Hope of living in a peaceful future
Seeks by all to rectify ignorance torture

Attitude

Providence has never let it change
On the contrary I have grown over hinge
In a free country with freedom of speech
Offer scope to know country's psyche
Confused childhood in wrong environment
Induced me by entering the young spirit

Outside influence never let me amend
Poverty ignorance comes with dividend
Surroundings make seeing things one way
Biasness strengthen me spreading sway
Reflecting in ones arrogance slowly
Received as sacred as I steer deliberately

Maneuvering let me never transform
Shrewdness becomes company in all form
Exposed in weird materialistic environment
Leading you to be critical of judgment
Taking all good away from the oppressed
I sustain poring rancor among alienated.

River

Summer heat create me at the high stack
From the frozen snow wrapped mount pack
Get secretly held by the mountain green
Insistent pouring force me down the incline

I move with fear some energy alone
Through the valley and the plane
More streams rush to join me on my way
Surging me wide provide huge gateway

Power within me wipes both banks down
Hate myself to be the reason of ruin
But my turbulent flow brings happiness
Amidst I meet up much of human needs

My flow not restrict into single boundary
Benefits dispersed amongst all and sundry
I find pleasure in human unification
But blocking me might result inundation

No state alone can claim on my water
As I serve all who lies on my manner
They share my bloom in their prosperity
As they share my bareness in their poverty

Every Body Needs Somebody

Bee has been humming for sometimes
Her voice not heard by companions
Flowers in garden are staring up to her
Need her presence for all bloomed there

Child needs parents for upbringing
Parents help child strengthen his standing
Aged parent crossing a road looks forward
Find humanity in some extended hand

Teacher teaches students with pious plan
Parting knowledge with his young clan
Obstacle and turmoil harass people often
The society needs incessant fortification

Hunger strikes as natural phenomenon
Prioritising as top human stipulation
People look forward to suitable remedy
Selfless farmers meet up this cavity

None decides who would help whom
Human rationality holds duty syndrome
Situation brings in best of humanity
The society survives cycle of eternity

My Fury and the Society

Every year I arrive with all my mighty
People failing to predict my potency
Travelling through a determined way
Brimming at many places I get away
Finding my way through low land
Houses and roads disappear into mud
Become reason of sorrow and destruction
I come back every year with sensation

Mitigating the loss of life and property
Distressed offered reliefs for sustainability
Much of the reliefs find way out to trade
Fortune fools needy who slip to be dead
Displaced resettle after water drying up
But flood havoc strikes next year sharp
Malicious cycle goes on before open eyes
Unscrupulous enjoy their yearly slice

My fierce could have been toned down
With a preventive plan in place made known
Money would not have found any slippage
As society saved life to get rid of savage
My enormous energy put to use for science
People earn health, wealth and its essence
I remain a natural phenomenon to assist
Healthy living mankind wishes to persist

A common man

I am a cart puller or a trucker
Carry goods from one place to other
We get remuneration
By delivering goods to destination

I am a farmer or a farm worker
Produce grains for our fellow member
We get paid by remunerator
On selling our produce to collector

I am a Grocer or a trader
We sell things to neighbour
We earn remuneration
By selling goods to our buyer

I am a teacher or a preacher
We educate all our dweller
We get remuneration
On finishing job of presentation

I am a Police or a Force
We protect our entire populace
We are paid remuneration
For providing job of protection

I am a fruit vendor or a vegetable seller
We sell fruits and vegetables there
We earn remuneration
In exchange of hard toil put on
I am a postman or a draftsman

We work among the fellowman
We get remuneration
In lieu of our services to the nation

I am a fisherman or a sailor
We catch fish or carry individuals
We earn remuneration
In lieu of services to our persons

I am a ticket checker or a traffic manager
We simplify lives of our fellow dweller
We get remuneration
In lieu of services to the nation

I am a soldier or a doctor
We fight against respective enemies
We get remuneration
By rendering services to the nation

I am a leader or a pleader
We split people on social order
We survive on cold money
By snatching peace and harmony

I am a minister or a decider
No one knows what we are after
People often doubts our integrity
We become subject to people pity

Am I a common man or a burden?
Less read and unfortunate mundane
No one assume our occurrence
But we exist in the human race.

King of the Jungle goes back

Animals of Jungle are not rationale
Some are strong some are frail
Stronger kills weaker and the meek
There goes the rule of Jungle we pick

People of the soil are rationale
Rationality divides people to fail
There is one King and rest his subjects
There goes the oppression as he likes

Unlike jungle distressed reunite
Each offering resistance for fight

Common rationality finds resonance
Society form movement of significance

Dislodgment process set in motion
People participate in this incineration
Scraping the pseudo nationalism
Throng spirit bury the opportunism

Who am I?

I have come from west going to east
And see human race but find only beast

In front of me there were rays of happiness
In mask of progress I resolve into madness

Starving and death do not influence me
I find merriness in the arms of supreme

I can walk anywhere without validation
Find time to spread hatred and detestation

Common man issues do not bother me
But I think out of box ahead of theme

Nation grown with faith in brotherhood
But I make it ruffians' playground

Got rid of the long blue of colonialism
I find mere opportunity for explorism

Derisory preparation force us backward
Foggy avowal fails me going forward

My dream remain on paper and media
Poor intellectuals make me run out of idea

I am neither an intellectual nor a visionary
I am a man as opportunistic as an ordinary.

Given a choice

Given a choice not like to reborn here
Wishing not to be a dispassionate leader
Lacking emotion for fellow country men
Spreading hatred misguiding often
Each forward step brings in adversity
Self- interest supersedes citizen necessity

Given a choice not like to reborn here
Wishing not to be a patriot farmer
Victim of neglect gets lesser priority
Proficient farmer skill becomes charity
Bad weather lower yield increasing debt
Cold governance prefer farmers' death

Given a choice not like to reborn here
Wishing not be a patriot soldier
Those given the task to protect the state
Self-centric power use it for own interest
Group not taking order from his superior
Forced to work in isolation by the ruler

Given a choice not like to reborn here
Wishing not to be an ordinary commoner
Doubtful eyes would follow you always
Treating you as a stasher or a rebellious
Every day would force a painful vow
Freedom less being always fear of ruse

Vindictiveness has no place

He came along with huge whack
Frightened subjects cries quack
Many leave places hiding themselves
Shouting and chest thumping prevails
Boasting his might came after the clan
Hurriedly put in place a diseased plan
Happiness ran over peoples' plights
Wrong diagnosis creates side effects
Instead of the deceased kill good cell
Pain ride on body agony wane soul
Indifferent to society downfall
Frightened subjects are sent to hail
Late came review of wrong doing
Try to pull back the deceased string
Whatever damage to occur was done
Fun of illusive gang went on the run
We ask who profited from the job
Opine citizen the right case for a probe
Commoner wonder what would follow
Word of change proven to be hollow

The governance

Once upon a time there was a realm
Ruling king fulfilling people wisdom
State prospered taking its people along
Liberty with peace made a proud nation

Then come a period of hostility
Unleash by a group doubting the liberty
Elected despot spread divide and hate
Trying to get rid of all what was great

New steps derision of people placed
Reaching nowhere soon irritate the head
Inapt measures that followed soon
Took the nation by shock before doom

Like the time of Sultan of bygone years
People were inhibited using own coppers
As if a legal plunder besieged all
Life whacked following the new fall

Imposing colossal hold-up for people
State termed it beneficiary to topple
When subjects oppose the coercion
State termed it treachery and sedition

To be kind and caring for the fellowmen
Teaches the benevolent art of governance
Providing equal opportunity for its citizens
Leads to success for the sustenance

Purposeful alliance with the privileged one
Would set up a society sick with disillusion
Before it is late when society stops existing
Unbiased governance is for humanity

Counting of heads

We live in a modern day
The Sun still rises in the bay
People stand in queue and wait
For their turn even come late
Wishing to draw own currency
For mitigating their grave urgency
It is the gravity of your requisite
Decides the length of the plight
Fall apart your normal living
You pay your price for trusting
More heads in the queue tells
How severe the super truth hails
Authority become egotistical
Play truant by turning primal
As if longer queue signal failure
Managing breakdown with stature
Counting heads becomes important
For the authority to be on target

Failure

Upon occurrence it upset
Mind run shorts of thought
One wonder world would end
Wishing for another bend
Coward attempts not to fail
But cowardice put him in tail
Arrogant tries to be smart
But arrogance fails him apart

Leader's failure is game change
For people it is lack of knowledge
Failing boss terms it innovation
For subordinate it is demotion
When leader fails the nation
It is unscrupulous surrounding
Failures do not teach lesson
Leader stay engaged in delusion

Sportsman fails to improve spell
Failure teaches lessen not to fail
Failure of student undesired
They warm up for working hard
Shooter does not want to fail
Making resolute in perfecting skill
Failure being part of development
It teaches art of improvement

Failure is a temporary deflection
Not an enduring apprehension
Key lies in tracing the reason
New effort will fetch in sensation
Empty bottle sounds much
Boastful imitator start from scratch
Never let failure demon you
You control events so success tow

Crossing of the Line

There is always a line invisible
We never cross it gullible
The line demarks our thoughts
Control our perception slip-ups

Many not knowing the line exists
Efforts to cross over it persist
Risking the live environment
It disturb semblance of ancient

Every effort of them fall array
Engaging mind to justify the parry
Intellectuals pinning the blunder
But arrogance whisked under

Let us limit our vision within line
Never cross it for the majority divine
Fulfilling the desire with reality
We should recognize the validity

Dreaming the desert I am crossing
But reality takes a severe thrashing
Unseen land we step in unplanned
Would cast severe agony prolonged

What if you have nothing to do

I have enough time in dispense
I move around on any defense
I shout whatever I have to shout
Even if it means nothing to most
I often say because I can say
Even it makes no sense what may

I forget I am to show the approach
Instead go after the past to reproach
Forget I embody you not an individual
But as your ambassador cultural
My saying matters where deeds fail
Making out speeches with grave trail

I imagine things in my delusion
Words that follow create confusion
Leader is who leads the group
Lack of faith in own ends in droop
To remain in limelight satisfy aspiration
One remain unmoved to exasperation

Chasing one dream after another
With no accountability to bother
Free bird I make people daydreaming
They dream flying high not knowing
Unhappy they fall in absence of reality
Nightmares that follow kills ingenuity

Frustrated community lose trust
Add more failures to speaker's hat
People memory is said to be short
Transitory they can be fiery and hot
There is no dearth of good past
One should remember own habitat

Day dreaming

He has taught me how to day dream
I feel unhappy as people dry stream
Time pass by dream comes false
Provoke me losing faith in my guts
Rebuke fate unknowing what is stored
Carry on with tomfoolery unexplored

Leaders teach commoner day dreaming
They do with a purpose of exploiting
You learn it from speech and publicity
But watchful study reveals its clarity
Daydream lacks sanctity for preaching
Soon it would turn out to be cheating

Daydream based not on facts but stunts
Attract our mind honest thinking blunts
Let us promise not to give in to its pity
Saving society from the future calamity
Falsifying some for glorification
Would not augur well with gratification

Sailing my boat

I have learnt to sail in river
Flowing one way make sailing easier
Easier sailing relieved me of a sigh
Up my social antenna I flew high

Then came selling in the Ocean
Piloting the boat become uncertain
Face difficulty in sailing boat safely
The wild Ocean shakes it unduly

Fact remained Ocean is unknown
I appear to my country like an alien
Not knowing the direction of the wind
I navigate on preaching with vague mind

Sailing in Ocean like running a country
Does not follow a specific data entry
As if state had in me the only sentry
Hundreds of civilians died in the past fury

I remained untouched floating in Ocean
My boat has not capsized thereon
There are turbulence and face off
People continue doubting my sailing stuff

Humanity & Nature

Sorrow of Mankind

Once there exists a celebrant
He preach as a way of extant
People speculate under its impact
Some liked the sermon some not
Opportunity puts him to lead
Very soon he became the head
For every single day he passed
Continue to ignore the distressed
Life of commoners suffered
Almighty above got annoyed
Droughts strike calamity follow
Devastations made life swallow
Large numbers ended their life
Poverty led rest carry on fight
Talk of development continues
Agony of mankind multiplies
Issues remained unaddressed
Life continued to be threatened
People wonder where it would end
God's annoyance continue to raid
Wisdom envisage senility triumph
Recurring con would not pass off
People would lead a peaceful reign
God would allow happiness to win

Bearded Seeker

Look is hidden behind beard and facial hair
No one is able to read person's face ever
Happiness or sadness never finds reflection
Arrogance though seen in many occasions
They have been the mask for many scoops
One wonders who take care of the holy loops
The person is in hunting for many years
Entities hunted are tigers' sometime dears
Many innocents die for no fault of their
Bearded seeker witness as the only viewer
Bent upon thou twisted hunting process
Love choose cow over oppressed innocents
Bullets pierce in to the innocent prey
Ensuing fear of life sends others at stray
Long flame rises from the blazed dwelling
Touching the sky through dark spiraling
Gradually whole society will burn to ashes
Shattered people will become homeless
Soon a multi-storey will find a place here
Poor's hutments will grow around there

Alien

Which planet you have come from
You have created psyche storm
You do not converse when required
But create noise when not required
You cannot justify your wrong act
Avoid by joking the grueling fact
May you name your dwelling?
Is it heaven or hail thy prevailing?
People like to pay you darshan
To exchange their sorrow and pain
Great Alien you are dear to many
Do not leave us for other nanny
Do not buy us arms ammunition
Rather give us food and nutrition
Allow country's wealth to grow
Make our own money to flow
Allow our farmers to be blissful
They produce food being skilful
Pay heed to discomfort and agony
Of the small marginal and tiny
Oh Alien you are a great irony
Country received you as cursory
Becoming bigger than what worth
Has put all of us in great dearth

Perspective

You are good in perceiving
Do well to jolt by immediate tackling
You lift the idea of the opponent
Put in place it by concealment
That is how great ball player survives
Captain drive team in all eventualities

You are good in planning
Promptly denounce what is succeeding
You conceal your plan of copying
Put in place old deed in new packing
That is how you overcome conflict
You lead the team against all argument

You are good in being uncaring
Do well to promote by lone playing
You listen to copy hiding your feeling
Find tactical ways for old score settling
Vengeance keeps you searching success
You start leading with meager passes

You are good in provocation
Promptly creep in high suffocation
Shift to adoration for mustering support
Put in place your less assertive rapport
Less in self-belief distract following rule
Poor point of view makes team ridicule

.

Who is He?

He who walks along with the poorest of the poor
He is the Lord

He who walks along with the one not meeting both ends
He is the Lord

He who walks along with the mother not able to feed child
He is the Lord

He who walks along with the farmer whose crop is ruined
He is the Lord

He who walks along with the child whose father is lynched
He is the Lord

He who walks along with the writer whose face is blackened
He is the Lord

He who walks along with the parents whose son is martyred
He is the Lord

He who walks along with the journalist who is threatened
He is the Lord

He who walks along with the child whose father died in the queue
He is the Lord

He who ensure all these sacrifices bring in change
He is the Lord

The Great Practitioner

Brainy practitioner has every solution
Unaware of the decease and the rationale
He provides remedy one not the right
Producing side effect no cure in his sight

Being the showman of the circus
Accompanied with assistants and whips
Try to treat the patient not the ailment
Disease remain alive killing the patient

People doubt your learning and ability
Following their rigorous pain and agony
Whatsoever tasks the doctor gets on
All go astray in the midway operation

Each failure accompanies with diversion
Lame excuses forwarded as Justification
Multiple failures weaken the patient
Live society undergo pity and discontent

Failed doctor will come and go away
Society in the shape of Patient would stay
Playing with people psych and emotion
Never be a road to success and solution

Eternity

Surrounded in the dense forest of Deodar
Edge of the steep Mountain View cater
From the uneven corner of the hills
Cascading sparkling water stream spills
Selflessly roving in its downward sprint
Creating many rocky water tubs in its swift
Rocky boulders try to hinder its way
Overtly increase its momentum of sway
Below at George it flow at high velocity
As if to keep its promise to infinity
Irrigating the soil through its passage
Spreading its solace on the masses
I wonder where from you get this water
You are flowing for ages together
Your exuberance offers life indomitable
Symbol of eternity exist inseparable
You not only charm my mind and heart
Looking at you alone my soul gets assert
Curved bridge on the river joins two sides
Likewise falling streams join two vibes
Seeing you for a while fails my satiety
Transparent drops brings out your purity
More I see you more I struck with gaiety
My soul wants to join you in eternity

Wound

A soldier stands to preserve sovereignty
Exposing him to danger to attain purity
Physical wounds make him ill critically
Aged parents lie in sore wound mentally
Human engineered enmity leads to rioting
Sending innocents to menace of slaying
Physical wounds make many ill critically
Seeing home in flame wound mentally
By falling from cycle kid hurt physically
A mother undergoes soreness mentally
Two lovers bite the dust of squabble
Each undergoes sorrow of being terrible
Outing trip snatch kid's life accidentally
Parents suffer bolt from the blue mentally
Pain either physical or mental does hurt
Both create sympathy in a human heart
Men insensitive to caring stop existing
Mankind inculcate sense of discarding

Hills have Eyes

Planet Earth has wonderful creations
Hills valleys plateaus and mountains
Top them with River Lake and Oceans
Positive ambient allowed life creation
With magnanimous hills in the north
Endless seas and ocean in the South
My country bounded safe and sound
Ample peace harmony in spell bound
Hills lure deep pull to fall in affection
Invite us often to be in their seclusion
People of hills are different from us
Honest life makes them labourious
People are their eyes lives their lesson
Hills teach us art of ecology protection
Hills see us through the time eternal
Our wrong doings are punished natural
Hills echo their displeasures through fire
They have eyes that works true sincere
Hills recognise greedy corrupt mighty
Punish them through quake calamity
Hills have eyes that recognise sincerity
Payback poor with affection and pity

Eternal waiting

She waits long for arrival of offspring
Together with the pain of carrying
She then waits for baby to grow
Many hope play hide and seek row

Waiting for husband return to home
Time pass by her in waiting roam
Child grows up and goes to school
She waits for her safe return home

Teen goes to hostel for higher studies
Adds to mother's waiting miseries
Half the empty day she stays alone
Waiting stands her only companion

Child comes back from institution
Higher study cut short the reunion
Her waiting continues hope peeping
Youth prepare in challenge seeking

Her ward soon joins the work race
She waits for ward to find a place
The cycle of her waiting continues
New era of ensuing change ignites

Wait in planning ward's life partner
Wildest dreams she encounter
Married child doing job stay away
Wishing to see them she waits all the way

She waited long for family to prosper
Seeking to end a happy life after retire
Her waiting however still continues
In eternal search for ward's happiness

Reality
&
Liberty

Numbering Mountains

Mountains are mystery to mankind
My country is bound by them all side
None has ever tried numbering mountains
It is like counting waves of the oceans

Mountains and rocks created naturally
Cosmos has no control numerically
It is amazing how big, scattered they are
Mystifying common land they share

A big mountain overlaps many small ones
Like a big scam cover much insinuation
Head lay the reason of subversion
Jointly the juniors carry out the execution

Counting of mountains sounds hilarious
Punishing scam star even sound oblivious
Nothing will make any difference
Scam remain mystery to human sense

Reign will come and go unaware of history
Manner of fiddling will be cursory
Newly clothed one would seek adventure
Dubious rule hides behind the past venture

They do not need our approval

Warm spring follows winter
Make our ambient warmer
Big trees shed old leaves
Get covered by new leaves
They are usual phenomenon
Nature needs no permission

Planets make the Universe
Moving relative to one another
Movement cause climate to alter
Spring then yields to summer
They are usual phenomenon
Nature needs no permission

Hot summer melts snow peaks
Creating cool water streams
Ocean rises to make rain cloud
Summer bring in rainy period
They are usual phenomenon
Nature needs no permission

People show Nature indifference
Plunging to seek undue license
Selfishness annihilate environment
Lies make future unholy circumvent
Nature obeys its rules meticulously
Devious human ruin rudely

Second Liberty

Parrot stares at the sky with a sad gaze
She is restless for sometimes in the cage
She witnessed many changes in the home
Events strike her memory in quick some
Pains and agony of people influence her
Being swayed she aspire to be a free flyer

Countries have witnessed hasty actions
Putting people life and wishes at coercion
Each day in their life become intolerable
Whole nation feels rigged through very soul
Country express regret over their blunder
Decides to propagate second freedom war

Liberty is what desired by one and all
A parrot or a citizen seeks to break the hail
Like caging a bird takes away her right
Snooping in public life create spirit to fight
It become a second war for liberation
Ensuing time carry freedom proliferation

Rulers do not take lesson from the past
Forget to honour the perception of trust
Thrust upon indecency in public space
Demoralising majority consciousness
Innocent secular citizen suffer disillusion
Country prepare for second liberation

You cannot overrule always

Everyone has a definite role to play
Howsoever small or big one may
Seeing ants carrying their ration
People learn about possible rain
Caterpillar build cocoon around
Cocoon provide great silk strand
Dog barks hearing strange footstep
Warn us to be cautious on doorstep
Sudden blaring birds in night middle
Alert us about the ongoing tremble
Jumping monkey scream shatter us
Hints the presence of carnivorous
Each one of us has some role to play
You cannot override endorsing a slay
Rulers think their power indissoluble
Ignore that pivot lies in common people
Pains and agony of majority commoner
Bound to destroy the self-centred chaser
Head cannot override the aspiration
Good sense prevents insubordination

Return of modern Shylocks

Farmers fall prey to local moneylender
For carrying livelihood as crops producer
Being cheated by the goons of retailer
Getting their earnings squeezed harder
Local musclemen force marginal trader
To part their hard earning as barter
Smooth working of the factory sustains
On the mercy of local antisocial rodents
Called modern day Shylocks all they are
They are created in collusion with ruler
When ruler becomes the bone of ache
Every morning adds new way of shake
Shylocks invent new way of robbing
Ruler practice policy on weak sobbing
Hard hit poor remain busy in struggle
Modern Shylocks amass flesh piping bugle
Devise the norms benefiting the affluent
Shylock in guise of ruler cheats the scant
Lost and deprived will unite in defense
People will triumph after due diligence

He who does not take pride in his History

Perhaps I know you Sentry
A citizen of my country
You do not take pride
In your country's past stride
You read country's history
As if it is untrue and cursory
You see the hand of unknown
As if he has connived along

You try an altered strategy
Out of your hate and jealousy
You distort and disrespect
It becomes your fancied treat
Your action sets the trend
It is the new fashion unwind
Renaming institution change stride
Truth of events fool historical bind

You feel often tiny and ignored
Before the eminence of the great old
Your lack of talent low devotion
Make you inept of conception
Lack of vision set in loss of glory
You fail seeing future neutrally
Actions guided by mistrust fail
Result sure to end in spitefully hail

Propagate large scale partisan act
Cause social discord to distract
Innocent people end up in turmoil
Doubt and suspicion prevail
Distortion of history is indecent
It sow seed of great discontent
Progress stops as deliberate
Society breaks into fragment

Hatred in you bring in to light
Events turn rigged seen in grave plight
Present world would keep a watch
People overlook your conspired dispatch
None would accept such a disaster
Your misconduct qualify slander
Every national would take pride
In his real past in sacrosanct stride

It is raining outside

Damp courtyard wet clothing
Messed up life all depressing
Skyline carrying cloudy haze
Drops on shed sounding rage
Potholes cause chaos on road
Guiltiest evade civic sword
Citizen moves on despair
Manager hides public stare
After rain brings in fresh air
Smog goes down with water
Dirt in the air stand cleaned
Brazenness of mind remained
Hypocrisy in open continue
People swallow the solitude
Privacy being meddled
Survival put intimidated
Outside rain clears the Air
When will our psyche get clear?

Quiescent State

State is sleeping under menace
Not knowing what it sense
Rains destroy our grain stack
Thousands remain hunger struck
Time play cruelty with us
Till it open our mind conscious
Worries lie should it get late
Faster must it percolate?
Fairness not seen in horizon
People cry around in confusion
Hatred climbing the life ladder
Mountain of indecency sadder
Minds tweet visions blur
People joining shameful slur
Ignoble person rising high
Society crumbles on its lie
Soon we get out of dozer
Before they ruin moral fiber
Silence thou name of ignorance
Longer it befooling conscience
Wait for a written surveillance
Before offering a public pittance
Time for nation to be upright
Apathy must get thrown out

Storm is coming

My brown soil warmed up
With all odium and rage
My clean air stands fouled
With all lies and hate
Earth cries in the void
There is none to vindicate

Warmed air goes up
Piled up angers lay trap
Overhead sky turns to black
With dirt of lust at dusk
Disorders doubts spin out
A storm is to break out

People are provoked clan
Animals placed over human
Producers of grain are dyeing
A perspective plan is working
Frustration leads to mistrust
Brewing storm is to burst

Forgotten dissent

Life has become art of compromise
Every step forward force to reconcile
Unknowingly becoming hypocrite
Hypocrisy becoming newborn's trait

Countrymen has forgotten dissenting
Insanity in most of them plagued in
Listening lies viewing half-truth story
Giving in to misinformation over glory

First time hatred percolating officially
Leader contribute in it significantly
It is working under a systematic plan
Antisocial network stood as ruler's clan

People were swayed by provocation
Not knowing the hidden co-habitation
The guild could never win people trust
Is allowed to enter the system crust

System allows it to grow like termite
Soon country gets bare from inside
Commoner get into worshiping cow
Before rich and powerful they bow

In the midst of forgotten rebellion
Country advance to autocratic union
Chaos anarchy prevail to decree
Introspection makes caged bird free

Fellow citizen

Proud citizen of this wonder land
Sages and greats glorified its sand
We lose interest in existing ones
But seek things not belong to ours
Ignorant mind prefer copying freak
Sway down in hypes of the shriek
Our opinion thinned on a chuck
We embark on gullible smack
Unseen pain unfelt agony revive
Laid out trap fail us to survive
We respond the call of the silly
To find us rot in future gloomy
Longer we allow this sick flock
Irreversible will be fall out shock
Prolong injury to social fabric
Silly adventurism bruises the basic
Despairs catapult cohesive repulsion
There must happen people revolution

Greatest Dilemma

Today what is seen is not the real
Shown thing is a corroborated deal
What you hear is not correct
Heard words appear never accurate
What you believe is not true
Fabricated belief reveals to be untrue
What is felt honest is a fraud
Fraud is never perpetuated by a god
Today slow train gets derailed
Thoughts of bullet train is a paranoid
Where a dead sweeper gets salary
How does it build a clean city gallery?
Here black gets white by a bank
Wiping out black appears to be a plunk
Perpetuator of genocide joins hand
How does peace prevail in sober land?
I wonder about differences do exist
Greatest dilemma appears to subsist

Team Member

You are a proud member of the team
Prevalent ambience testing its esteem
You were happy as team was doing well
Cannot be uncaring when it is in turmoil

Toughest challenges would be set
Lucrative offers infuse your mindset
Loyalty should navigate your judgment
Divert evil spirit by the past good event

More wiliness should be the guiding logic
Morality be replaced by people ethic
Cadre to clash the civil war tooth and nail
Leader to ignite lost passion in the trail

Evolve ways countering point by point
Raising each of the scam of the opponent
Propagate their futile acts costing nation
Highlight from top to the downtrodden

Unity is the strength not to be forgotten
Imbibe loyalty to be the winning devotion
Bring in honesty eminency to the core
Convey the nefarious con design to the fore

Censure

We blame other when we defer
We feel won when we fail other
We make merry not in glory
But in common men's worry
There is no glory to take credit for
Seed of success sown by pioneer
Standing upright is cowardice
Adapting psycho fancy braver dice
Blaming the past becomes fashion
Hide your failure in comparison
Define untimely death as fashion
Living in fear now a propagation
Reign from far is order of the day
Poor people lives under dismay
Truth gets reprimanded by design
Such is the practice termed benign
Qualification loses its meaning
Under pretention of overriding
Biasness finds new designation
Ability is replaced with adulation
Games of musical chair prevail
Befooling of commoners sail
Blaming previous not wins ever
People watches sly even keener

There is Darkness outside

Grave floods seized much of the land
Faraway places are abandoned
People under misery fights for survival
Dearth of shelter paining all
Same water being shared by the corpses
Of many colour and creeds
Floods have united them in the death
Leaders failed them in breath
Nation floating on water minister flying
Dead child on lap mother crying
End of grave misery not in urgent sight
There is all darkness outside
With sleazes country is full to its brim
Twisted ruler's game not in trim
Individual corruption is supplemented
By mass fraud in policy made
Deceitful planning done in darkness
People mistook fraud by fairness
Floods damage with transitory haunt
Will pass of as annual sacrament
Trick of deception being perpetuated
Will leave deep sore fabricated
Nature wishes its justice prevail soon
People reassess bliss over goon
Affluence getting amassed in a few
Deprived slips in disparity due
Outside darkness bound to be deepen
More lives oppression laden
Worth of lives ceases its significance
Inequality gets in abundance
Powerful content in rising divergence
Make merry of poor prudence

Perfect Hero

My hero will be one in many
In arrogance he is uncanny
In secrecy he is selective
In duplicity he is seductive
In lying he is second to none
In evading he is the perfect one
In bullying he is hostile
In apathy he is like a reptile
In behaviour he lacks decency
In despair he shows lunacy
In setting up he is diligent
In diversion he is intelligent
Human value bears no relevance
It is not in his cup of conscience
Manmade disasters do not pain
Racism tops his list of disdain
He is my Boss the perfect hero
Subordinates decry ill destiny solo
Two rising hands divert my mind
Make me wonder what is destined

Wish tears in your eyes

Uncertain about your destiny
Played slaying as your symphony
Not able to win their empathy
You snatched their sympathy
Arrogance is your chest belt
Has built in you as an ornament
Deception is your orientation
Has effectively created detestation
Your actions raised mass pain
But you remained busy in disdain
Symbol of two-facedness
Set scores under fake kindness
You are king of the kingdom
Let your crooks pick target random
Your actions fool fellow member
Chariot of jealousy ride on divider
You continue pebble picking
But infinite ocean beach never ending
Hypocrisy will cease paying soon
We pray for strength in unity boon
You have never felt a crying soul
Wishing tears of repent your eyes roll

Struggle

&

Pain

Fighting a War

This is the war against inequality
Bring to light the state of disparity
Rich busy in wealth apportionment
Poor still alive is an amazement
Wealthy are dealing to get richer
Deprived fighting to remain floater
Hypocrisy sold out to prosperous
Through the means of staged census

This is war to survive physically
Bring to light the hatred implicitly
Long ago earth created the first life
It went under cycles of survival strife
Infant fight making its presence
Baby's cry seeks to show intelligence
Grown up fights for their stature
Corrupts unite to cover their failure

This is the war of social endurance
Bring to light the design of pretence
All are engaged in fighting hostility
Confronting perpetuator's proclivity
United we would watch our step
Let us not fall in the laid out trap
Success lies not in withering the past
But in learning lesson out of that

Making of a Star

This fellow would play a lead role
He is a human with roguish soul
No less than a Nero people swear
He raises coming from nowhere
Nation embraces many people
They work on senses arguable
Fanatics often play with their nature
Making them of short sighted stature
Unable to make out truth or false
People get swayed by cheap hypes
Fellow citizen fix the fate of the star
He will ignite ramp by words spar
Hoodwinking of the country men
Becomes a regular mean to entertain
This star being built with duplicity
Hypocrisy in soul become simplicity
Wishing to win laurel in global case
Fail thou people in humanity race

Criterion

Word qualification is a mirage
You ran after it cause outrage
You need not to be competent
To race in the success of ascent

Where economy run by advocate
Welfare done by greedy merchant
People cry for safety and justice
From the pain of lynching malice

Nation branded as full of juggler
Many street wolves roam in hunger
Daughters are unsafe on the street
Influential few busy on tweet

Outsider did bloodbath in the past
But they become ruler here to last
Same tradition rolling on in our day
Carnage perpetuator crowned today

Criterion do not merit any longer
Art of terrorising approved to linger
Scholars get their face blackened
Midnight sees adversaries raided

You are freed today

People faith placed you there
A monument of history to share
Overlooking us from a high
Remain all the years' as time fly
Summer winter you stand tall
People pass by you respectful
Your act created our history
You freed people from misery
Thoughts ideology wins hearts
You rule over mind and wits
Progress got right direction
With equality and co-operation
Then came a black storm
Of hate jealousy and division
People fight amongst themselves
Ruin the peace and semblance
Worst days bring in adversity
Demolition serge in secrecy
Social balance lost harmony
Crook dislodge you in hegemony
Even stony bust did not escape
Being lynched in open landscape
You are freed as a historical cue
On a black day of grim and glue

Lies are Out

Lies have only one religion
It is fake that is day's sermon
They are preached as tricks
Turn people to become sick

Telling lies form the habit
Child grows to become addict
Slowly form his attribute
Adult rhetoric adds in salute

Lies can never be hidden
Evil mask soon stand torn
Wishes behind lies are not real
Dreams plant on lies peril

Lies often come in package
With foul rhetoric language
Dancing caricatures stoop
Lies wrap speaker in a loop

Lies are out often this day
Morality dies on the pray
Actor never stops his act
Inferior folly drags his tract

Dreams become irrelevant
When sown by an arrogant
Worth swapped by smartness
On bed of deceit lye usefulness

Long Drive

Spring has come early this year
Cuckoos shrill has cut short winter
About two third of life is used up
Never realised it would be so fast

This long I was deep in work
True side of life has lowly struck
Retirement has given spare moment
Face true agony of living torment

That was time I engaged in toil
My interaction with life was gentle
Free time revives childhood craze
Life's rhythm falls back to graze

Mid-life stress pains me realize
Why aged wants to be sage rest of life
Most difficult period of life it is
Searching reason for subsistence

I would come across two minds
Naturally surrounded every moment
Feel like going for a long drive
Where the road never ends in oblige

Real pain

Coolness of winter passes of quickly
I remain confused with grime reality
Spring solace cold with its warmth
Of the hard life unforeseen so forth

Responsibility and duty never ceases
Man is asked to continue his services
Forced to complete his entire obligation
Till his last breadth dies in exhaustion

Complexity of mind adds to pain
Shocks pollute soul unable to regain
It is not life one ever dream at spring
Desolation to individualism bring

When wishes not harmonize mind
Body do not match steps with side
It is time I need to reassure myself
Life's real pain takes care itself

At spring man wishes painless living
Residual time in the midst of cheering
Realism reserve the other way
Real pain lies in facing in the sway

Ice will melt one day rivers would dry
Pain of spring would last as long man try
The real pain subside superseding time
When my ears and eyes stop mime

Pain

It is four letter word "Pain"
When it touches heart shaken
Spasm silence my mind
Sobs dry the soul inside

Memories bring tears into eyes
Inside feels a vacuum of cries
My belief in faith dries
Longer agony pervade bruise

Human soul is a neutral entity
Carry on with sensitivity
Grow inside a beautiful mind
Hear its call when in tide

Search inside your soul
Before you indulge in foul
A beautiful mind show you way
You hear weeps in your sway

Justice cries

We look up to you when in trouble
Your impartiality assure us in console
Purposeful mind let you down
Ambiguity surrounds your gown

Justice is always above suspicion
The other name of God's audition
Lead you to betray the truth
You surrender morality set forth

Malignant mind make you a prey
Soon the cancerous venom spray
Crooks promote seed of dishonesty
Making justice fixed and dirty

Unfairness roams free on street
Justice wanders in bias ambient
People are helpless in her absence
Justice itself cries for liberated essence

People are proud of sovereignty
Untainted ambient enjoys dignity
Sacred autonomy get to be must
Healthy prudence bring back trust

What is in Store?

The kid is playing on the street
His face is brighten as sunlight
Unworried about fate of the day
Happily engaged in the play
Father not knowing what in store
Gone to factory in his routine chore
Mother works as housemaid
Keeping dates with her regular head
Both return home hands empty
Lack of cash takes them to cavity
Omen of bad time suddenly appears
Spiteful governance put them in tears
Unable to pay fees bring uneasiness
Unable to draw ration put them in distress
Normal life of the family is upset
Not aware of what is stored in their fate
Discomfort threaten the small life form
Bigger fish swims back to sea bottom
But there would exist supreme saviour
Big ones be netted by the God for sure
Relentless pain and agony make one hard
Time will arrive for finding move forward

Beast among us

There is always a beast among us
Luck as it be not aware of the fuss
It waits to come out in commotion
Social disparity form the condition
Gutless leader spoil people synergy
Commoner is sucked of the energy
Hate and jealousy pile up the heat
Peace shrinks letting envy up built
We find them in the history page
Notorious stories of oppression rage
Daya River witness the dreadful saga
Remember bloody war of the Kalinga
World witness the brutal annihilation
Jalianwala air cried seeking protection
Rudeness a state of mind of living being
Turns ugly ejecting our monster sing
Once out it leaves spell of disasters
Present time witness many such blunders
Massacre of Gujarat bleeds our heart
Slaughterers went on rampage apart
Muzaffarnagar left many shelter less
Lynched Akhlaq made Bisada helpless
Burning alive of Bishop Stain
Remind gory story of human swine
We muster witnessing ugly exposure
But overlook the beast within ours
Repentance never seen in perpetuator
Inside creature ride on spreading rancor

Eternal Remembrance

I was staring at the blue sky through the window
The red-flowered tree dwindle her shadow
Reminding me of the noon you were teaching lesson
Mother you had chosen teaching as profession
I remember you travel by boat crossing the Ganges
Daily you reach your dear school in the odd village
Sharing family burden you enabled us grow
Life of you served as great motivation we owe
We reached our destination foundation you laid
Mother we remember you in gratitude wet eyed
I was not on your bedside when you breathed last
My heart today is not in sync with mental state
I always remember you when I am in problem
Your faith and belief guide me overcome them
Mother you are always in our heart every moment
Eternal remembrance always stayed resonant

Civilisation
&
Relationship

Girl and the Little Duck

Group of ducks swimming in the river
Young girl was playing by its rear
Seeing the ducks she was wondering
How beautiful creature they being
In the group was a beautiful little duck
Accompanying the mother duck
Playing hide and seek with her mother
They were free to go any where
Soon little duck fell back from the squad
Entangled in the bushes of the river bed
Young girl jumped on the water stream
Rescued baby duck holding close to her arm
Soon the group of ducks had long swam
Separated little duck was safe in cozy arm
The girl becomes her friend in quick turn
Sometime after she decides her to return
Ventured in searching the lost Group of duck
Putting the baby duck in her backpack
She and friend walked along the river bank
Evening slide to night spending in boat trunk
Next day located the lost group of ducks
Nested in Small Island created by the junks
Jumped in the river carrying the baby duck
Swimming along with her reach the pack
Mother duck recognise her baby with quack
Jovial baby duck swims back to mother duck
Heaving a sigh of relief seeing their reunion
Young girl goes back with sweet emotion

Squalor

Society is full with dirt
Filthy smell in air spurt
Mental decay all around
Tricks as facts going round
Lies hum so brazenly
Ears feel tired echoingly
Dried river bed fall mercy
In greedy crooks fancy
Covetous burn hill forests
Flood churning God directs
Standards fall every sphere
Human life gets meager
Rumour takes innocent lives
Empire covert plan survives
Human live face uncertainty
Ruler sells mirage with gaiety

When naked lie surface its head

We cannot misrepresent history
By distorting facts in cursory
When we try hard by mixing lies
People learn the purpose behind this
Common people can be fooled once
Historian will fight with vengeance
Propagator of lies will not be forgiven
People will identify them to be forsaken
When intention becomes dubious
Ruler cannot wear a veil of odious
Power in you force your deception
Degree of lies will decide your ambition
Misdeed often punished for violating trust
History will treat lie mongers with mistrust
Governance is transitory in nature
But truth prevails is enduring in stature
Our past is glorious irrespective of sight
Distorting it for vengeance fail its spirit
Let us repay debt to history we inherit
Civility is not in altering but taking pride in it

Art of tricking

Foe of the poor friend of the rich
Part in between is made sandwich
His day starts with a calculation
How to set the art of strangulation
Disappointed with value erosion
Events follows exploit the diction
Building was due for improvement
But it ruined the original basement
Future of the house sling in danger
Architect engages in new blunder

Lack of fund puts house in disorder
Unable to prioritise the order of repair
Ugly state reaches the point of chaos
Luckily God send his Milking cows
We seek its blessing whenever needed
Our house refills with wealth heeded
Too much taxing kills the milking cows
Fund flow dried stopping work of house
Borrowed money spoils the bonhomie
Art of tricking leads to point of gloomy

Running train falling prey to accident
Death does not concern our sentiment
Leader dreams of riding on elephant
People have tasted suffering in pant
Spoiled by juvenile plan and poor vision
Country's resources are put on auction
It is not my house but the name and fame
Art of tricking aims the depth of our pain
How long the country bears this agony
There should be an end to this symphony

Sharing

I am Nature created your world
Blow wind which you share
Create Sunshine in which you soak
You cannot deprive us I rock

I am nature teach you civilisation
Bring awareness among population
People share benefits of welfare
You cannot divide us I dare

I am nature imbed in your facts
Teach truthfulness amongst sects
People learn co-habitation
You cannot poison mind I caution

I am nature nurture your form
Motivate people joining social storm
Society learns bond strengthening
You hear best human trait is sharing

Relationship

Human relation is strange
While alive a few valued presence
On death near one die within
Outsider shed tears not knowing

People do not stay together
Not because they forget each other
But they stay together
Because they forgive each other

Relation is a true alliance
Works on principle of endurance
It continues so long it is wanted
Remain alive till longing lasted

Love dominate even after death

Love is not strident
It does not announce its advent
But it leaves void and pain
When it is fore shaken

Love is a self-centred act
Does not follow outer world tract
It signal mind to be possessive
When emotion is left uncreative

Love dominate even after death
Lover wishes on her dyeing breath
To be buried under a flowering tree
Flowers rain on tomb at the cemetery

Love becomes the only companion
Keeping alive mental union
Life passes by in its stride for the rest
Wishing two souls join at the earliest

Hate sells Love not

Human being hates to be hated
But feels good accepting hatred
Spreading odium is like winning war
Surged revulsion forgo care

I see world dividing amongst two
Seller of hatred finds easy clue
Love does not find many takers
True that needs honest receivers

Hatred gives short lived gain
Scattering of it does not make rain
In the long run hate unlock
Baffled people will face the shock

Let us not give into abhorrence
Good sense tries to test tolerance
Interest guides one accepting hate
Revealing the lies will fumigate

Humanity is the garden of the nation
Beliefs and views tart its intention
Ambience promote selling of hate
When truth and love annihilate

There exists a difference

You look up with apathy,
While I look up with sympathy
You work for the privileged
I throw myself for the deprived
Your eyes throw boastful arrogance,
My eyes seek modest humbleness
In the air you walk to foil
My feet find coolness of the soil
You confide in division
I find pleasure in unification
You take pride in pursuing coercion
I find happiness in liberation
Fear mistrust prevail among populous
Leading a difference between us
You make mockery of our past glory
I take pride in our history
Ambition runs ahead your capacity
Securing mass confidence my priority
You have found mastery in direction
I stuck to ground realisation
You walk with sycophants around
I walk among masses on the ground
You are my Boss seek obedience
I wish to be lucky making defiance

Why you hate when I speak truth

I told truth when I was young
No one believed me then
People now hate me on
As I am now grown
That always I lie now
But people seriously bow
Habitually I distort fact
People merrily clap

Country did not believe then
When it was young
Statesmen believe him now
When the nation has grown
Six words put a society in turmoil
Citizen start doubting its soul
Core prayer of your own
Seen robbed in the open

Hateful mind cause harm
As the society was young
Now the country bleeds
As the nation has grown
Clubbing lies piece by piece
Ignoring genuine needs
Rudderless boat sway
Goes down with its foray

Imprisonment

What you did you need protection
So many guards loop fortification
Remain caged in your own creation
You indulge in soul purification

Fear of loss appears in your dream
Sitting standing chant death syndrome
Hymn of threats has set in your mortal
Threatened mind cause soul to derail

You talk about hostility every where
Remain unseen of cruelty in own sphere
Most people languish under poverty
You seize their hard earned satiety

We face difficulty in meeting both ends
Jobless youth roam on road dead ends
Progress of the society has long stalled
Monetary disparity grown enlarged

Unkindness stood facially augmented
Each day new avenues being persecuted
More you try incarcerating populace
More you get imprisoned with disgrace

Ideology

Ideology plays great role in person's verve
It separate people in to group reserve
It divides people with certainty
By its very nature leads authority

When it leads to assume power civilly
Ideology tyrannises democratically
Principle, belief oppose co-operation
Inevitable division comes out of rotation

Ideologist is not a person with seriousness
As he will never see the consequences
Conflict of ideologies leads to agony
Society undergoes destructive tyranny

People volunteer in absence of authority
Teamwork leads to success of superiority
One assumes authority in lie disguise
Never bring about a world order legitimise

Chameleon changes colour

Chameleon jumps from one branch to other
Swiftly adapt to the new branch colour
To suit new ambient is its natural ability
Changing body colour matches its duplicity

Indian media once known for its boldness
Never compromised their independence
This day truth has surrendered abjectly
Like chameleon changed its colour swiftly

Today's media sponsored by outside fund
Agenda being forced by unknown hand
Out of fear journalism has forgotten its oath
Twisted falsified it presents lies and half-truth

There has started race among them openly
For pleasing the lord of the ring shamelessly
Having forgotten their responsibility to society
They have become society's bonded apathy

People wonder where has gone the honesty
Journalists dance at the whims of psyche
Chameleon change colour it is their nature
Journalists surrender truth in whose favour

Disrupted civilisation

In the guise of expansion
Hills are subjected to annihilation
In the name economic progress
Rampant deforestation is in duress
Uprooting of forest rupturing of hills
Severely confront common wills

With no purpose in the familiarity
With no facts on the soil hydrology
Ill planned endless blasting of rocks
Resulting harsh sliding of land blocks
Locale lives worth low in their concert
Willful distortion fit their resonant

Hills of the north and the north-east
Safe guard our existence and the zest
Nature has made them tricky terrain
Hindering city bustling keeping it serene
Hills have different mode of civilisation
Life is nurtured by nature preservation

Hills would endure and survive longevity
If we let them bathe in natural prosperity
Let us not bring in anymore disruption
Civilisation does well in preservation
Let our leaders understand the truth
Ill policy leaves much derogatory myth

Hope
&
Indecency

Line is thinning

Under clear sky free bird flies high
In democracy new idea heaves a sigh
Autocracy censure idea to shape on
Despotism never allows idea to be born

Today country is under turmoil
Helpless citizen targeted by open troll
Perspective plan will strip individual
Solitude would make soul suicidal

The line is getting thinner and thinner
In the absence of a strong drummer
Venomous snake stands out of control
Killing by suspicion dodge rule

Disparity between death and existence
Getting leaner in the designed persistence
Pruning tactic shorten social order
Road roller shame to humanity crusher

Narrow thoughts gets further simpler
World will get rid of humanity rider
No respect will shine your ability
Thinning line end up in soul insanity

Right is always right

Truth is what is right is always right
Eternal sunshine is always bright
Falcon sees it right from farther
A dog recognise right his master

Right thinking leads to right action
Deceitful thinking yield subversion
Plan biased with lies scheduled to fail
Cunningly conceived one sure to derail

Mischievous learning never yield right
Arrogance glorify fool's plight
Adapting cunning means fail to succeed
Vindictive mind shun friend in need

Learning right thing in right way
Often get your laurels in certain sway
By shunning arrogance and meanness
Pave way for good human kindness

The Dawn

Dark night ends in a clear dawn
We pray new morning to be better one
Veracity stored for us however differ
Each day start with loss of a soldier
Followed with the rape of a minor
Child get assaulted by the molester
Daylight shines adult murder at lodging
Noon perpetuate a cold blooded lynching
Scary night kill the penniless firm trader
For selling his aged cattle to a purchaser
Night media gets in hated discussion
Dusk worry how citizen would live on
Unsure about agenda of the next dawn
We get up praying for a better one

Joker of the Century

Twenty first century is on the go
World has survived the silicon woe
Our nation marched ahead in decade
Putting depression tears in to cascade
Plummeting world economy affected us
Brief slow growth made us cautious

Circus of calling the bluff originated
Citizen did sink in the trap contrived
A human mind is fond of dreaming
Cruel joker exploited the truth griming
People swayed by the flabby thoughts
In the midst of absent of fighting guts

Joker has won in tricking the spectator
Arena is facing the grave precipitator
Gloomy show down continue to go on
Spheres of life touched fell to move on
Waning keenness yielded redundancy
Perverted eagerness create indecency

Threats of hatred stiffen road ahead
Distrust filled air caused all disgraced
Cheater's attempt to cause laughter
Momentary it cut our mind as spoiler
Society runs on the noise of hoodlum
Joker would find none in the podium

Union of Minds

Marriage is often union of two souls
One tries reading the other in console
Union of minds create a mutual goal
By merging two individual souls
New goal seeks to usher in happiness
A family is born out of keenness

Union of mind shorten if souls fail
One cannot read others in counsel
Failure of soul leads to confusion
Seized minds undo new creation
A family is never formed
Partners prescribe a separation

Separated being is like an animal
It sees happiness a plot dismal
Indulge in ideology affiliation
Hide arrogance in despotic action
Failed soul gives in to split vision
Dissect society on wealth and religion

Barefaced Arrogance

Memorials built by young emperor
In loving memory of beloved dear
Glancing at it induce fondness
Of moments of shared happiness

Stood on the death-beds of innocents
Kingdom often reminds the tyrants
Killing innocents to become rulers
Carnage ensue victory of invaders

Country boasts of the tyrant
At the cost of tears of the torment
Oppressor goes high on free orbit
People made ignored and forfeit

Ruler indulges in distorting history
Plot to replace facts with invented story
Stamping own name the brazen act
Shamelessly show arrogant tact

Lonely Mind

Thoughts would like to go back
To those good old days
But that was not to happen
Soreness appear again and again
Imaginary psycho infecting
On ruse flag their ugly wings
Ruin peace and somberness
Hurt mind tries hiding loneliness
Once spread love lose impetus
Broken physique search solace
Age roll on quicker, mind ruin
Me not a god only a human being
Lost love makes me lonely again
Cruelty of words cause pain
Heart gets beaten harder and harder
Shameless utterance comeback stiffer
Lonely mind crawls on happy time
Wants to fly in bright sunshine

If I could see future

We do not know what is in store
People would love to know more

People cannot see their future
Deprived would love to prosper

One do not know the next target
Would it be a poor or an insolvent

Under privileged cannot cry
Their fatigued eyes ran tears dry

Black cloud over head brings rain
Twisted mind make things uncertain

Adversaries prevail in disguise
Society is haunted by surprise

I wish I could see the future
I can save people from the butcher

Vanishing Humanity

Humanity is in scarce today
Bigotry is in full display
Compassion is a lost word
Loyalty is often misplaced

Fading kindness left voids
Making most people restless
Blacksheeps are on stroll
Society live in sore turmoil

Leaders often shun politeness
Coddling people for nastiness
Shielding the malice action
Wiping out social fabrication

Fellow citizen can never be this
Something wrong in the paradise
Society has lost its harmony
Fading humanity its hegemony

Forgotten dissent

Life assumes an art of compromise
Each step forward force to reconcile
Unknowingly becoming hypocrite
Hypocrisy becomes newborn's trait

Young countrymen forget dissenting
In them lunacy have plagued in
Blatant lies viewing half-truth story
Given in to humbug over glory

Hatred fast percolating officially
Leaders contributing significantly
Working under a systematic plan
Latent peril obliterate majority clan

Student protests human insanity
It was easy for them fight hypocrisy
Work force burdened with despair
Debt ridden never be dissenter

Forgotten to laugh

Once you appear in my dream
You were not in happy stream
Unknown wrongs creeping worry
Making you unfocused in hurry

Keep on rehearsing old verses
Cannot switch often your devices
Lies are out in open quietly
Doubts visit many mind silently

Ill-advised traveler stops often
Recurrence of mistakes is certain
Setting Sun fails to encourage
Shaken confidence ceases leverage

Arrogance in deep drives attitude
Lies often spiral around the statute
Worries suck fun out of your face
Have forgotten to smile with grace

Inauspicious day

That day was an inauspicious day
A modern Shylock was born on this day
There were tremors storms everywhere
Temple bells rang in high pitch fear
A strange alarm rang in mother's ear
Newborn's life vexed her mind in fear

Country got freed from the oppressor
People settling down with successor
Ignorant about sacrifices of the ancestor
Young boy turned into a fellow basher
Grown in the troupe of odium advocators
Sermonized as one of the hate preachers

Followed the path of abhorrence ideology
He mastered in separating people's identity
Adoration cohabitation replaced by division
Riots propaganda forced mass isolation
Innocents handed over destiny in shock
Hated ideologist emerge as Modern shylock

Misrepresentation

He never exhausts slurring
Nor he would stop lying
Habitual misleading his bluff
He is caught often in puff
Make people to day dream
None of which ever in stream
Every act a frantic afterthought
Pursue hollow aimless purport
Dispensing national heritage
Using as if his own baggage
Motif behind every action
Find pleasure in vindication
Action never meets our need
Doomed state bears the misdeed
Travesty continue to be shoved
Bemused state stay ill-advised
He is one of the many members
Selected as my state councilor

Love for Religion

Everyone loves one's religion
Forever close to one's oblivion
One preserves its solemnity
Feel proud of being in eternity

Love for other religion is nobility
Noblemen promote respectability
One reading is far less to know
A life exhaust often to follow

No one learn religion on hearsay
One to follow through heart way
Superficial learning kill humanity
Interfering with life fails sanity

Hawker fake love for religion
Deviously percolate delusion
Bigotry inch society to anarchy
Religion never teach to be muggy

Colossal wastage

The Saryu River appears burnt up
By the lights of the thousands lamp
Water reflects with scattered beam
Bottom remain the darkest stream
Scared wealth spent on human whim
Like a mad Sultan's perverted gleam
Scanty resources killing innocents
Owing to inadequate breathing airs
View sordid state of mental sanity
Hapless people search human pity
Deprived of the least health care
Survival needs force poor to dare
Ecclesiastic ask for refusal of action
Noble profession infuse dedication
Brazen craziness should surrender
Before the blue state turn a howler

Indecency

Whenever one look around
Everywhere liars are found
Sheeting lies in the society
Much like birds in the party
Cowards often roam in groups
Without job they form troops
They are growing like termite
Plowing through backer mite
Lives unsafe in their yarn
Mob lynching a matter of turn
Never know when it perpetuate
Kin is left broke as it permeate
Cries of deprived echo around
Thrashing lesser god get ground
Fortunate preach social decency
Leaders coach activists' lunacy
Indecency appears every stem
Rooted in the fabric of the realm

Vulnerable Future

Welfare

The word welfare has become defunct
In the midst of Indian observant
People life stands invaded by oppression
Open harassment follow no reason

People welfare has no place in notion
Intent of doing lacks imagination
Pains and agonies of mass vibrate in air
Showing apathy hardened the ear

Good and simple a vague corollary
Spun out of biased uncaring glossary
Trade in chores of disarray annihilation
Welfare cries about the air of oblivion

Wellbeing is not a mere word
Nor a festival stunt publicly lectured
It is a ground reality to be felt by people
Comfortable citizen would feel agile

People welfare is a mission
Undertaking it needs zeal and passion
Hypocrisy will not allow it to succeed
Fizz of deceit leads it to be failed

Chasing Ghosts

Thousand ghosts are awaken
Dancing on streets embolden
Black western sky seek justice
Ghosts thrives on blood rinse
Mid-night gloom wrap ghosts
In opportune time slayer thrusts
After gory event ghosts vanish
Clean chit to ghosts add blemish
Governing spirit separate human
Fixes its target by secret action
Ghosts prefer to pick its feast
God given bloods similarly taste
Our ghosts born out of hatred
Keep in race for making divide
New class is secretly born here
Ghosts are blessed by the ruler
Fighting the green every where
Added ghosts pouring there
Lack of will making it difficult
Chasing of ghosts falling flat

Power Flies

Governance has no heart to beat
No ears to hear no eyes to sight
Barefaced gimmicks are its wheels
Incessant deliberate slur its fuels
When Shylock made an accountant
Sucking poor is the art he learnt
Resentment prevails in society
People cannot express free parity
Authority shies of downtrodden
Power flies high with face hidden
Folks are helpless before leader
Feel cheated as they hold power
Power restricts people decision
Alms evade targeted population
Power flies high ignoring meager
Allow it hiding behind despair
Poor governance looks for alibi
Power driven arrogance shy

Remembrance

You took the role of my mother
As she was a school teacher
It was period of your learning
But had to take care of sibling
You sacrificed your education
Completed upto matriculation
Being elder got married early
Went to make your own family
I remember you were very daring
Crossed the Ganges by swimming
Killed deadly snake hitting by stone
Handled rough and rowdies alone
Fell from roof chasing monkeys
But you survived with God's grace
You took care of us with amorous
My elder sister you were precious
You left for heavenly bode long since
I remember your caring to cherish

Wisdom of Crowd

Evolutions made us to be rational
Sovereign thinking is relational
Rationality leads to sovereignty
Sovereignty create sense of liberty
Liberal citizen tend to feel rationally
Wisdom thrive in moderate mentally
Moderate citizen form majority
Crowd wisdom prevails in a city
Irrational people loses sovereignty
Fanaticism thrives in the society
Citizen shows high intolerance
Man-made tragedy gets into dance
Radicalism sway ignorant brains
People engaged in avoidable strains
The society loses peace of mind
Disobedience flings in the wind
Crowd wisdom gets polluted
Hollow growth story hallucinated

Bad things do return

Youth run after glare and fantasy
Tends to go astray for ecstasy
Brazen lies of showmanship
Kills their belief of pioneer ship
Education replaced by loitering
Dejected involves in crooking
Society once got rid of bad things
But they are back on this morning
Bad things accompany ill destiny
Bemused society engage in fenny
Terrorising people form abuse
Mental pain accompany the obtuse
Residents are rid of their dears
A few arrogant cowards sneer
Create new generation vigilant
Vengeful turned jingoist abundant

Restlessness

The dawn yields to a bright morning
Assume this day not to be depressing
But for your hankering after attitude
You disregard diplomatic amplitude
You lower your esteem position
Often you ruin country's reputation
Arrogance drives you to high claw
Your wiliness and lie make us bow
Citizen look up to your confidence
But joke behind for your ignorance
Hero you are but you fail us often
Realm suffers pain that never lessen
Restlessness melts in your ambition
Not knowing the future outcome

So much noise

There is so much noise around
Everybody speaks loud
No one listen to other
Truth goes under cover

Mad man talks to self
Unmindful of what it feels
Wolves howl in unison
There goes luxury illusion

Honest priest discourse
People hears with apt notice
Follows in real life silently
But in privacy individually

There is so much noise around
People hides in shroud
Dark cloud hovers up above
Blank future seal the move

Chaos surrounds us all day
Confused people loss way
Noises scare our opportunity
Liberty heave of humanity

Symphony

Dark clouds hover up around
Stalled mind put work ground
Future of the day not assuring
Bleak progress often haunting
People do dance in symphony
Often unknown about irony
Veiled reality smears great bluff
Strives matching untruth stuff
Freedom projects past good
Fortifying our brotherhood
People read in lingo of terror
Fear of loss fails raising order
Apathy allows nonstop bully
Power hides against quiet silly
People in symphony continues
Busy in daily choir pursues
Sea in turmoil grabbing the land
Slowly symphony cease to wand

Unforgivable Sin

You possess the burning desire
Acquiring other person's wealth
You concoct devious plans
Against your innocent clans
With the intention of robbing
Their dreams, hopes and ring
You drift towards sinful shark
Consciously forget the good track
You walk on the path of evil
Tell lies intending dignity to spill
You engross in acts of violence
Against weak and innocence
Burn their property and dwelling
Cause harm to women and children
You hurl insults and abuse teachers
Criticize ancestors and martyrs
Sinful acts never go unpunished
As our Lord oversee the deceased

Forgotten laugh

Chasing the long life have taken out my shine
Do not know when it has quizzed my smile
I have almost forgotten my regular giggle
Laughter is like withdrawal cash from machine
Sometime we get some more often us not
So uncertain has become our routine spot

Searching laughter we walk in the park
Artificial laughs in assembly we try to crack
Huge wasting of time we do not mind
Lord from above chortle in post hind
Pain of life has dried out our smile
Grin from farmer's face has been docile

Vendors van stands in the corner empty
Scant cash disallow him sell in gaiety
Many minds are scared of unknown fear
What will happen tomorrow for pain to shear?
Never thought such thing would happen
Life's laughter would fade away so certain

Unclear Apparition

One bad fish makes whole pond muddy
All the good fishes suffer being trashy
Louts are allowed to rise on the road
Making each life exposed to be mobbed
Aged and young none are spared
Fall in the russet eyes of the crooked
Being set as the trend the society turmoil
Folks fear their lives going to upheaval
Force people spend days in worries
Qualms surrounding them as miseries

My Country

My India had lived in country side
Glimpses of tradition made its ride
There are thousand tiny villages
With all lively and happy faces
My India is unreachable at many
In spite being twenty first century
All muddy roads lead no where
Lost in the event of long shower
Darkness increase their hardship
Basic needs still play mischief
Bullet train will run in the city
Farmers continue to hang in pity
Mislaid priority engulf my country
Becoming famous top the psyche
Best part of country still deprived
Future of most remain deceived
Modern age failed my country
Answerability belied by the sentry
Failures take him behind excuse
My country moves on bemuse

The Adjudicator

Once called the gentleman's game
Growing distrust on Umpire had it tame
Good sense put a third one on the two
Whose decision become binding on duo

Wish it come about in today's society
Where citizen doubt the Supreme honesty
The one supposed to deliver fairness
Allows falsehood win over truthfulness

Disillusioned citizen roam around
Seeking justice in the name of God
Manmade judge laughs on the lurch
Wish a third adjudicator carry the torch

Sewing the Nation

Winter has spreaded its wing
Covered the enter swing
You me all felt cold pinch
Homeless look for trench
Poor adults find no work
Roam in the uncertain dark
Ruler busy crafting darkness
Making people defenseless
Chalking out path of progress
Leaving mankind in disgrace
Through distortion and lies
Shaping national psyches
Left-over freedom deserts
Nation is sewed by perverts

My Religion

I do not have a single religion
It is a matrix of multifaceted canon
Beliefs, philosophies and tradition
Form pillar of its foundation

Built on myths of cosmogenesis
It follows humanity as eternal hypothesis
Compassion constitute its only mainstay
Fairness integrates in a neutral say

Eradicates hatred from emotion
It builds on forgiveness and passion
Simplicity openness forms willingness
Follow to imbibe its tenderness

More people would see its grace
They would come forward to embrace
A new world of peace evolve prosperity
Where all share common sagacity

Role Reversal

Work he did now being done by other
Aim to pay him with his own ragger
That worries him making him quirky
Disgraceful words lit up his face perky
Forget handily he did the same action
Disjointing folks was his holy creation
Alienated minds seep deep into the soil
Blood doubt water while both spill
This summer is scorcher than past one
Indecently wrapped in hate and odium
Tolerance testify people for their limit
Intolerance comes into flower tight
Find in oppressed people the respite
Role reversal would then be complete

Great Escapism

You are mother of innovation
Art find new ways of deprivation
Comparing throws open opportunism
Thou is art of great escapism

Lonely scream find no ears
Helpless body put to shatters
Matter judged as normal pessimism
Thou is art of great escapism

Burdened poor lose expression
End his life in utter desperation
This event termed ordinary pessimism
Thou is possible art of great escapism

Broken Promise

You promised to hold my hand
But you travel in a distant land
You promised to walk down with us
Your adventures make you mysterious

You promised to hear people voice
But garrulous spoof suit your poise
Your one-sided talks create Holocaust
Your promises remain broken steadfast

The land made you to be a person
You got free voice for coercion
Broken promise swayed the nation
In to a split up culmination

Reality is not written in a book
It is realised when you are on foot
Moving in the company of reprobate
Broken promises cannot surrogate

Expectations

Future stored is wounded
Lesion decaying within
Intoxicating mind rapidly
Odium venom spreading freely
Human society stand crippled
More people getting incensed
Places for remedy blocked
Covetous souls stood sold
Tyranny spreading wings
Tyrant let loosing gremlins
Resolves seen misplaced
Wits stopped looking forward
Society in state of shrubbery
Expectations hiding in bury

Shifting of Beasts

Beasts are changing their place
No more restricted in forest dense
Become visitor in nearby town
Hunting their livestock down
Beasts as well seen in the city
Terrorized people look for pity
Seen feasting their ways merrily
On them high blessing pour freely
These beasts are not from jungle
But from illicit poacher's stable
Always spewing out hatred nasty
Using the language of vulgarity
Beasts hunt meeting their hunger
Media beasts preach as slayer
Shifting beasts struggle in plight
City beast reside amid us as termite

New Sky in the Horizon

Dark sky wants to set free
Nowhere birds can fly free
Ground is filling with corpse
Of human lynched and torched
Invites hunter for dissection
Vultures filling the sky horizon

Stained sky wants to set free
Society tries to be rid of mockery
People trapped in selfish game
Suspect each other without shame
Sky is not blue any more
New sky in the horizon roar

People will not tolerate open shits
Preach by corrupt and cheat
People will drive away evil spirit
Plurality in diversity comes to re-exist
Country will stand reassured again
A new sky appear in the horizon

Mistaken Notion
&
Social Agony

Stalled Decision

Small hamlet lies on a beautiful valley
Bounded by long mountainous gallery
Peace loving folks happy and healthy
Looking forward seeking prosperity
Thaw out cold streams flow bluish
Meadows rip open freshly greenish

Human mind is like an open book
Wishes are written on what you look
Present day mind tremble in polity
Mind in dilemma lacks rationality
Bunch of rogues whip up passion
Loathing finds easy way in sojourn

A decision was taken a long ago
Wicked minds professed to sow
Diverted minds reap faded focus
Misled people live in ruckus
Split society lose legacy harmony
Heritage banish in to catastrophe

Adoring minds thrive in diversity
Brings in harmony in the Society
All beautiful minds resist dissection
Open hearts try stalling the decision
Unfair mind never thrive in affection
Humanity stalls the crooked decision

Weeping mother

Her ache was very deep
It has sadden her to weep
Tears roll down her eyes
Sacred drops endure price
Her tears are very precious
Falling tears are outrageous
Warm tears force us to swear
To remove cause of her tear

When son is killed in the front
Mother cries within her heart
A daughter is insulted in society
Weeping mother loses dignity
Open sky often get darken
Nation's patience get shaken
It is time taking vow upright
Address weeping mothers' plight

Wrong Design

Human creates rosy hopes
Take us too many dream stores
Try to sell delusions as many
So good in designing uncanny
Careless of unprivileged ones
Creates well planned derision
Pitiable will soon disappear
Deprivation compete hunger

Human do spread odium
Louts are quick to bedlam
World stand engulf with lies
Ability to see the truth dries
But truth in all nefarious lies
On own merit come in to light
A wrong design for mankind
Woven deep destined rescind

Sour Mind

Learning teach to look upward
Live with dignity mind forward
Distortion create empty soul
Mistrust and lie soon play foul
Every lie is contagious
Put erudite mind to be torturous
Human mind is instinctive
Coloured tartness grew in it
Innate mind beastly receptive
Being prejudiced and addictive
Sour mind fail in acquaintance
Missing wisdom forbid conscience
Fire never set at on its own
Outer force require for ignition
With continuous acidic utterance
Sour mind yields to arrogance
Honesty leaves simple soul
Simple mind turns to fowl

Look Inward

People around live in despair
Every moment is spent in fear
Crowd terror grew new normal
Roaming slayers free informal
Sign of law turn imperceptible
Cries echo in air dishonorable
Socio fanatic moving upward
It is the time we look inward

Lot of muck has flown into river
Get rid of it else it becomes driver
Muddy water inert and unclear
Annihilate all life and plants there
Country's vision like filthy water
Looks backward to compare
Nation progress going downward
It is the time we look inward

Black Cloud

Black cloud hover around
Create cool breeze abound
This is nature's generosity
Its way of calming humanity

Uncaring turn to other side
Deprivation goes north side
Black cloud yield heavy shower
Flood the nation in to tears

When injustice rule the roost
Nation goes into unrest
Black cloud reappears
Punish domineering rulers

The Imperious Ruler

A person is known by ones deeds
Perceived by company one keeps
Other will decide what oneself is
Not that what one preach of self

Imperious ruler speaks unsightly
Showing character unknowingly
Would love to draw comparison
When nothing works in precision

Hollowed perception lead failure
Diversion become the conjecture
Spreading lies become new rule
Obscure nation suffer ridicule

Officious ruler fancy arrogance
Prefer despotism over sustenance
Citizen voice suppressed by lout
Haughty enjoy the divided snout

Silent Killer

Leader flies preaching lies
Crowd surrounds man dies
Society mourns over death
Conviction spreads breath

Situation deteriorating fast
Leader busy keeping it to last
Social fabric under threat
All pervading silence spelt

No need of declaring a war
A simple lie made a predator
Lie spread faster silently
Killer mob do rest obediently

Technology invaded privacy
Bringing home human tragedy
Maintaining a studied silence
Will craft monster vengeance

Your Birth is a Lie

The bud came into being here
When water was everywhere
Life grows in full bloom
But it flourished into doom

With flood come much filth
Receding water stuck them in plinth
Foul ambient does prosper
Unwanted dirt flourished there

You come into being as person
Contagion hallowed in illusion
Chaste soul deflowered openly
Turning it to poison brazenly

Broken harmony failed demise
Scared mind never compromise
Peace fraternity not in pie
Your birth turned to be a lie

The Lake

Lake water is stagnant
However big it's mordant
Gets colour from its content
Many shrub and hedge plant
Lake bound on all side out
Foul water cannot spill out
With rain gushes huge water
Surround gets flooded over
Mucks swell adjoining locale
Foulness smack the whole

Like a foul lake it existing
Confined within spitted toxin
One steered clear of it knowingly
Saving long their soul candidly
Trying a few times flowering
Empathy barred from reaching
With sham came insolence
Delusion replacing resilience
Locale smacked with loathing
Ensued a ridiculous standing

The Comparison

A failure incite for comparing
Mislaid despair looks for hiding
Run away from truth perpetual
Awful comparison gets habitual
Escapism from failure fleeting
Factual truth remain enduring
Sham hollowness echo in the act
Factual logic stands side tract
Comparison as a diversion ploy
Used by crook pursuing to destroy

Comparing not a two way event
Excuses link past with present
Comparison is a wear of evader
Worn by the loser on falter
Biased soul prefer comparing
For their every wrong doing
Society never know the reality
Remain baffled in ambiguity
Comparison can't fool long
Truth prevail its winning song

Dirtiest Rogue

Century witness many rogue
Some famous some in vogue
Most countries nurture them
One or two turn up in helm
Environment polluter they are
Forest and ecology destroyer
High they go up with blessing
Brings in calamity happening
Social rogues like blood sucker
Often high in number they are
Blessed they turn to perpetuator
Dirtiest one embezzle the poor
Purposely hatch wealth detour
Beastly shrewdness is his rector
God even hate making a rogue
Today we have many in vogue

Living Reality

Fear of death hanging over head
Like a sword made of hatred
Biasness craft bad objective
Yield actions ugly repulsive

We are living in Dracula's lair
Full of sham and slayer
Venom emitter present within
Naive die by emitted toxin

Bounded in fake syndrome
Falsehood spread like drone
Suspicions separate each other
Innocent fall prey to imposter

Dreams embezzle nation aimless
Uncertain future people clueless
Each day open with new slogan
Deflated day end with detestation

Lonely Butterfly

Alienated from her flock
Tiny butterfly flying alone
She had risen over her shock
Flew over rosemary and gone

Whole life spent in singing
Stay dutiful in pollinating art
Tiny life teach us counseling
Shun hate shine in helping hurt

Felling trees annihilate wind
Warm up the earth ambient
Flora fauna fragrance bruised
Upsetting eco-environment

Overgrowing eco-imbalance
Wiping out these tiny lives
Tiny butterfly lonely parlance
Would soon end tiny promise

Innovative Decree

Realm does not need folk to rule
An innovative process play bugle
New set of army is associated
A new decree stand propagated

Digitalization supersede hunger
Even dead not safe any longer
Learning no more decide future
Sprite perpetuate eventual decider

Novelties take ahead game plan
New ideas do churn out of turn
Implanted into the national fabric
Furthering divisionary technique

Set of sham stalkers play around
Empire merrily thinks future sound
Bent upon the tremendous wound
That is inflected on the nationhood

Innovative decree venomous deadly
Would poison national fibre greatly
Brotherhood would stand tore apart
I shall not live to see much of that

My Society is in pain

Cries of Justice echo around
Realm seen flew its tail bound
Tardy trains laugh at us cruelly
Thrilling speed a joke morally
Rusty ruler talks of development
Nation sees as void statement
Expansion of road and cowshed
Respect for human life is dead
Son shoulder mother's corpse
A sordid state of health circus
The lack of roads severe village
King rally on multilane road age
Produce rot for lack of storage
Nation goes hungry of shortage
Each plan guided by main adage
Make rich richer poor disengage
Villages deprived of basic need
Colossal fund for park and greed
Serving people never was the wish
Claim to be a servant rub a bruise
Cries of destitute do not penetrate
Need a lynch scream to perforate
Nursing people prime responsibility
Private rogue enter due to inability
Commoner aches increasing daily
My India is growing backwardly

Habitual Rebuke

Hatred or arrogance both mind's state
One is urbanized other an in-born trait
One corrupt mind the other fabricate
First create criminal other perforate

Low in knowledge high in arrogance
Combination leads to over impudence
Mind tend to depend on info-prudence
Hollowness comes forth in severance

Hatred inside arrogance in chest
Turn one's skin thick and indifferent
Fear of failure and embarrassment
Leads one walk over a thin life vest

Censure become part of mind-set
Mind tends to spread faking contest
Regular scolding become habitual
People perceive the concealed ritual

Mysterious Hatred

How does one hate so much?
One cannot be indifferent so much
Thou soul is full with odium
Emitting this long pandemonium

Thou source of detestation
Ii is a mystery of indignation
Thou born as a common man
Hated too are fellow civilian

Crooked mind fears darkness
Prefer to spend amidst richness
Wilding vigorous lies as arsenal
Try to hold position irrational

Picture speaks

A picture would say hundred words
What would thou picture share
An architect of innocent carnage
In disguise of animal patronage
A picture of unscrupulous psyche
Debt-ridden farmer opt to suicide
Unleashed pounce of oppression
On low underprivileged section
Falsify as a saviour of humanity
Lead the extinction of community

What more thou picture would say
A selfish self-seeking arrogant gay
Always fit into few fortunate's ploy
While majority destined to destroy
Learning institute cease to survive
Behind wealth healthcare would hide
Amassing of wealth by chosen foe
Disparity amid have and have not grow
Much words comes of thou picture
People wishes to forget as nightmare

The Great fall

Rubble stones surrounded us like high walls
All our efforts to come out fall
We have fallen deep in the degradation ditch
Darkness in all spheres of life pitch

A fool with small heart suffering insecurity
Suddenly raised against the gravity
Group of Shylocks got into people lifeline
Turning the country in tragic vine

The great fall is swallowing us up like snake
Crushing moral fibre with freak
It will soon cripple social energy and stamina
And leave with us its entire stigma

Social fall is dividing the nation above reproach
Chaos deprivation soon to encroach
Time is ripe to make ladders of human column
We will succeed resisting the falter on

Standing Upright

&

Disenchantment

Time for paying back

Today we stand on free land
Gifted by martyrs loved hand
Great to be indebted to mother
Give sense of happiness at par

Rulers have wounded this land
Time and again she was disband
A few robbed her many a time
Pillaging persist too in new time

Great few given back time to time
Creating monuments and shrine
Ensured long peaceful cohabitation
Evolved human value orientation

Modern ruler plan people division
Hope to reign through polarization
Terror threats never win hearts
People will develop defensive guts

Time to pay back soon arrive
Resolve for coexistence survive
Payback will be a great whipping
By the means of traditional churning

Sarcasm never pays

Human mind is always restless
Often gets confused regardless
Grief turns it to sadness instantly
Joy restores happiness promptly

Doing sarcasm a sign of weakness
Use the void in others foolishness
Confused mind cackle in isolation
Eject momentary shallow sensation

Rogue gets sarcastic in open forum
Unscrupulous breaks all decorum
Sarcasm plays marvel in hiding truth
Listener forgets agony quick forth

Sarcasm blossom in mind deceitful
Being used as barrier purposeful
Listener mind gets into digression
Stupidity wins by truth suppression

Master practice sarcasm as a tool
Make his innocent subjects fool
Citizen recognize inner necessity
Sarcasm never pays any gratuity

Detachment

More you hate people
People will hate you
More you tell lies
Lies will detach you

Distance gets longer
Road ahead gets stiffer
People defy you more
Space to hide wane for sure

Distortion of facts hurts
Defiance seeks to lurch
Scared innocents withdraw
People detachment to grow

Unaware about driving
Why calling people for riding
Vehicle itself on broken wheel
Unsteady steering end thrill

Fairness

I wonder you exist only on paper
Meaning often ignored and severe
People fail grasping the reality
Damage is already done to society

I wonder how lies replace you quietly
Narrow mindset expressed covertly
Wider game played in your name
Rock the humanity in the shame

I believe you do not exist in reality
You were the last pillar of morality
People talked about fairness
Are living in cold mortuary helpless

I realise in the game of survival
Death only wins by cowardice ritual
People lost courage to raise voice
Fairness hides against cruel choice

The Truth

One likes to play fairytales
Make us to imagine happy dreams
Other show us the hard reality
Portrait degradation of morality
In between dies the eternal desire
Each one forgets loving each other

Barefaced lies cover the country
We are following them in paltry
Lie mongers unleash darts
Divide society in many parts
Person throwing odium exist inside
Why then search one from outside

Lies all around

When I look around I find air full of lies
Lies are so foul poison my mind as it cries
Pet go into hiding uncaring master's voice
Distorted media, unfair justice add to noise

Lie monger spread untruth in aid of minister
Rogues lie following a designed sinister
Lies propagate fast undoing social relish
Ruler's ingenious acts making police impish

Games of lies echoing around as if to honour
The vow of prejudice and apathy succour
Familiar lie mongers keep poaching our mind
Disenchanted neighbours suffering destined

Where there is smoke there is fire say the adage
Likewise each lie lay the seed of social damage
Puckishly stirred lies do not help win hearts
United consent will bring to light nefarious acts

Western Wind

The Sun is setting at the western coast
Foreigner's ships touch the shore post
Colonialists arrive with full gunny
Establish their tents numbering many
They lure locals with weapon and gun
Greedy locals in lieu gifted their terrain
Western wind allow foot of colonialists
Greedy few sold country to fascists

Today we live in sovereign land
Same tradition continues in highland
Few arrogant heads made friendship
With privileged selfish showmanship
Handing over fortune in their hand
All of our resources and precious land
Human greed knows no language
Dictated by crook's corrupt vintage

Dusty smoky petro wind from west
Gory ignorance of the north zest
My country in the hands of buddies
Society dies of pain and atrocities
Western wind has hardened its grip
Setting fascism to run the broad scrip
Being irrelevant in war of emancipation
Subjecting the country to suppression

Shattered Dreams

Emperor eats when he is in mood
Hungry poor not even gets one food
Access of good health and education
Has become a distant hallucination
Peaceful life and social merriment
Replaced by torture and punishment
One anywhere is asked about one's creed
Semblance of disbelief walk freed
Sensible education for average class
Accompany the dream of a middle class
Education and health run by the moocher
Dreams of the middle class run shatter
Every sphere of life is in grip of rupture
No one will be spared from being torture
Emperor sleeps when country fight
Shattered dreams struggle all day and night

Guilty Society

There was tranquility in the air
People were aware of their future
Peace and prosperity were prevailing
Truth of happiness in soul existing
Then came the historical blunder
Mischievous minds gather together
One lie after another whorl peaceful air
Create a vortex of mistrust and despair
People were swayed by delusion
Become guilty of historical allusion
Insinuation on people fate follows
Society bears the brunt of gallows
People were made to kill each other
Mistrust blossom in fright and fear
People felt cheated and raise voice
To find them as the detested choice
Poor people pay through their being
For the mistake and guilt society bring

Dracula's Castle

We are living in Dracula's castle
Not knowing when society face a debacle
Imaginary Dracula comes out in night
As they can't tolerate daylight
Today's Dracula is groomed in poison
Carry a few rings of protection
Each night ends in an uncertain dawn
For a tomorrow brings a new repression

We wish to come out of the mess
But spiraling into the vortex of disgrace
Losing our character and identity
In the veiled hands of Dracula's vanity
Today's Dracula is out of odium
Socially redundant heads pouring venom
Creating a day of vicious wrangle
It would confine us to Dracula's castle

Creating homeless

They are living in this country since long
Older they are we did not even born
We are uprooting them in selfish vow
Powering to protect seed of hate we sow
Pursuing our furtive game plan with tact
We make them homeless and redundant
Helpless they remain a second class citizen
To lose their opine power as denizen

God has assigned space for each one of us
We are to receive what is due to us
Homeless they are but not hollow like us
They will survive through scheme erroneous
Hard working human they produce grains
They form man power source in agro-train
Making poor as pawn in the game of religion
Will lead to anarchy and subversion

Condemnation

I find one criticising all about one's past
One censure all past good things that cast
To condemn or to revile become a habit
One creates around a detestable orbit

Our past had been good in all spheres
Good past enabled our secular bring ups
Colossal arrogance incite condemnation
Spiteful habit emerge out of connotation

Criticising never pays in the long sails
Condemning too never bring one laurels
But habit leads indulging in blame game
Games are played in reciprocating lane

Dancer blames the stage for his failure
Like the present blame all the past tenure
Frenzied denounce of past not augur well
Self-respect citizen do not bring you laurel

Worsen Ignominy

I see a kid behind every cry I hear
Unaware about the surrounding fear
In cry kid's pain finds an expression
Helpless he seeks desperate attention

When a mother cry her heart bare
With her child lying dead in front of her
Her innocent son has just been killed
I see a disgrace of humanity by evil kind

World of conscience narrowing its zest
Giving way to ignominy shaming the rest
Lord I do not wish to hear any more cry
Save us by forbidding social algae pry

Salutation

Country has lost most of its glory
Due to recent many acts of perjury
As the leading saviour of democracy
The world recognise our supremacy
Our respect for constitutional integrity
Was praised by the world authority
Country's honour for civil liberty
Reverently copied by all in gaiety

Today country is in remorseful state
Citizen pray for getting rid of spate
One neighbour doubt the other
No one knows what is stored there
People have suffered in all spheres
Leaders remain spiteful and severe
Past glory of unity in diversity is lost
We in century of fearful living of worst

Drifting away in the Sunset

Age knows no boundary I wonder
At the end of the day I surrender
Living happily long in the glorious past
Got molded suddenly to horrendous cast
Previous has always been encouraging
Present of late is extremely disturbing
At sunset gory of darkness lengthening
Not thought a sunset be so menacing
Meager savings of the poor is sighted
Quality of poor's fund been doubted
Painful face of poor and insolvent
Slowly drifting me away in the sunset

Do not doubt my integrity

Do not doubt my integrity
I am your history preserve gritty
Try not to alter me with tricks dirty
But submit to me in all solemnity
I am widely and wildly powerful
Shared by both honest and shameful
Cunning emperors got a place there
Through repressive acts of their
Good kings too made a place there
Through benevolent acts of their
Modern age leaders spread odium
They stand thrown out of podium
History has no place for crook
My integrity force me to overlook
Keep me as clean truthful as possible
Allow new making from being gullible

Time to Purify

Lot of dirt have flown in to my river
Discoloured it has given in breather
Mucks have begun poisoning ambience
Life ecosystem struggle in silence
It is time to cleanse the filth
Let the river come purified and stealth

Dirt trying to settle on the shelf
Making the surface grimy as we sniff
Strewn dusts fly in air and ambience
Making the society sick in silence
It is time to duster the rack
Let the shelf be back as shinning pack

Lot of hate has been spread
Each pious soul plagued disheartened
Poison swelled to reach the mind
Being expressed in anarchy destined
It is time to silent the hate preacher
Let each head rise in pride and pleasure

Indifference

Love for Power

Human being loves for Power
Wish to ride on the Eiffel Tower
Boat on the river Seine
Spend the evening in dine

Power build up tricks
Draw together impish freaks
Holding on to power liven up
Common interest backs up

Indifferent attitude inspire lust
Going with the way it destruct
People in power often overlook
Power derive vigor from crook

Aspiration sets examples
Many would follow it as temple
Country would carry the cost
Lust for power continue to post

When Monster troubles

A monster was created long ago
Turned our good faith in to rogue
We were restless for a change
Disparity widened the civil tango

Soured faith brought in darkness
Social quandary inked by the breeder
Civilisation ran into jeopardy
Future slips into wilderness

Youth aimless, society rudderless
Many jugglers lead to predicament
Rogue holds traps under sleeve
Progress become clueless

We created the monster knowingly
Being fooled country faced turmoil
Fooling continues unabated
Poor's wealth switch hands deftly

On its way to be historical distorter
Confused mind facing uncertainty
Desperation leads to nowhere
It is time to chain the monster

My meeting with fate

How many poor persons I ever met
Probably none silly may it be I bet
How many poor boys I ever helped
Probably none truly it be I hesitated
How many poor farmers I ever met
Probably none really may it be I bet
How many pained mothers I ever met
Daughters of who stood brutalised
How many ill-fate fathers I ever met
Whose sons were lynched it is I felt
My meeting with fate lies in dark
I did not speak for poor in the mark
Fate has never been kind to insolvent
Country lost glory in social indecent
I met with fate decided by well-heeled
Over the interest of the poor deprived
My meeting with fate lies in fabrication
Desire for power shun human inclusion
When enemy is within the country inside
Let us not look out for one outside
My fate represents that of million poor
Broken dreams made them fail to roar

Stopping the ruin

Whatever you touch turns to black
What you speak returns as smack

Societies bonded by love and trust
Masked utterance spread spell fast

Put on the path as torch bearer
Aimless loses strength and vigor

Teleprompter works for a while
It ruins program when it is stale

Knowledge passion guides winner
Empty container sounds drummer

Services to deprived disappearing
Replaced by on payment shopping

Nation being put to profiteering
Public wealth being rigged for feeding

Social degradation finds sustenance
When ignorance hugs arrogance

Let us not slip away the chance
Stop the ruin is the forbearance

The Cowardice

Death always distress human mind
Natural as human soul is basically kind
Grief does not differ individually
It comes from bottom of mind caringly
Cowards never lament but fear
Immoral past would follow them after
Fear of rebuttal makes them horrendous
Subsequent acts becomes atrocious
Cowards fail differing truth from lies
Honesty lose meaning before cowardice
Known dishonest is less harmful
Pseudo honesty makes society shameful
Weakness is an individual nature
Turns to cowardice after misadventure

Waiting to see the New Dawn

I foresee a world to be based on humanity
A world that would be guided by sanity
Where people of all religion, caste and creed
Happily move hand in hand worry freed

Children would unite parents at day's end
Parents hug them thanking God for being kind
Blue sky would look more shinning
Dark shadows on the soil would be vanishing

Human honesty and audacity would win
Over human misery, denial and deceiving
Someone would emerge as the leader
Holding flag of truthfulness and candor

I would live to see the new dawn
A dawn that contentment would sown
Adoring my past for showing path of future
By nourishing the poor and the meager

The End